King Richard the 2nd

By William Shakespeare

Edited by Julien Coallier

Copyright Julien Coallier 2012

All Rights Reserved.

Scenes

Act I – Page 9

Scene 1: King Richard II's palace. (Lon**don**)

Scene 2: The Duke of Lancaster's palace.

Scene 3: The lists at Coventry.

Scene 4: The court.

Act II – Page 43

Scene 1: Ely House.

Scene 2: The palace.

Scene 3: Wilds in Gloucestershire.

Scene 4: A camp in Wales.

Act III – Page 79

Scene 1: Before the castle. (Bristol)

Scene 2: The coast of Wales. A castle in view.

Scene 3: Before Flint castle. (Wales)

Scene 4: The Duke of York's garden. (Langley)

Act IV – Page 111

Scene 1: Westminster Hall:

Act V – Page 129

Scene 1: London. A street leading to the Tower.

Scene 2: The Duke of York's palace.

Scene 3: A royal palace.

Scene 4: A royal palace.

Scene 5: Pomfret castle.

Scene 6: Windsor castle.

Characters

Abbot

All

Bagot (Servant to King Richard II)

Bishop of Carlisle

Bushy (Servant to King Richard II)

Captain

Duchess of Gloucester

Duchess of York

Duke of Aumerle (Son of the Duke of York)

Duke of Surrey

Earl of Northumberland

Earl of Salisbury

Edmund of Langley (Duke of York, uncle to the king)

First Herald

Gardener

Green (Servant to King Richard II)

Groom

Henry IV (King of England)

Henry Percy (Hotspur)

John of Gaunt (Duke of Lancaster, uncle to the king)

Keeper

King Richard II (King of England)

Lady (Attending on the Queen)

Lord

Lord Berkeley

Lord Fitzwater

Lord Marshal

Lord Ross

Lord Willoughby

Queen

Second Herald

Servant

Sir Pierce of Exton

Sir Stephen Scroop

Thomas Mowbray (Duke of Norfolk)

Act I, Scene 1

King Richard II's palace. (London)

(King Richard II, John of Gaunt enters with other Nobles and Attendants)

King Richard II: Old John of Gaunt, time-honoured Lancaster.

Hast thou, according to thy oath and band, brought hither Henry Hereford thy bold son; here to make good the boisterous late appeal which then our leisure would not let us hear against the Duke of Norfolk, Thomas Mowbray?

John of Gaunt: I have, my liege.

King Richard II: Tell me, moreover, hast thou sounded him, if he appeal the duke on ancient malice, or worthily, as a good subject should on some known ground of treachery in him?

John of Gaunt: As near as I could sift him on that argument, on some apparent danger seen in him aimed at your highness, no inveterate malice.

King Richard II: Then call them to our presence; face to face, and frowning brow to brow, ourselves will hear the accuser and the accused freely speak.

High-stomached are they both, and full of ire, in rage deaf as the sea, hasty as fire.

(Henry Bolingbroke and Thomas Mowbray enter)

Henry IV: Many years of happy days befal my gracious sovereign, my most loving liege!

Thomas Mowbray: Each day still better other's happiness, until the heavens, envying earth's good happen, add an immortal title to your crown!

King Richard II: We thank you both, yet one but flatters us as well appeareth by the cause you come; namely to appeal each other of high treason.

Cousin of Hereford, what dost thou object against the Duke of Norfolk, Thomas Mowbray?

Henry IV: First, heaven be the record to my speech!

In the devotion of a subject's love, tendering the precious safety of my prince, and free from other misbegotten hate come; I am appellant to this princely presence.

Now, Thomas Mowbray, do I turn to thee and remark my greeting well, for what I speak my body shall make good upon this earth, or my divine soul answer it in heaven.

Thou art a traitor and a miscreant, too good to be so and too bad to live; since the more fair and crystal is the sky, the uglier seem the clouds that in it fly.

Once more, the more to aggravate the note with a foul traitor's name stuff I thy throat, and wish, so please my sovereign, here I move and what my tongue speaks my right drawn sword may prove.

Thomas Mowbray: Let not my cold words here accuse my zeal, it is not the trial of a woman's war, the bitter clamour of two eager tongues can arbitrate this cause betwixt us twain.

The blood is hot that must be cooled for this, yet can I not of such tame patience boast as to be hushed and nought at all to say.

First, the fair reverence of your highness curbs me from giving reins and spurs to my free speech, which else would pass, until it had returned these terms of treason doubled down his throat.

Setting aside his high blood's royalty, let him be no kinsman to my liege, I do defy him, and I spit at him.

Call him a slanderous coward and a villain which to maintain I would allow him odds; and meet him were I tried to run afoot, even to the frozen ridges of the Alps or any other ground inhabitable; where ever Englishman durst set his foot.

Mean time let this defend my loyalty, by all my hopes, most falsely doth he lie.

Henry IV: Pale trembling coward, there I throw my gage, disclaiming here the kindred of the king and lay aside my high blood's royalty; which fear and not reverence makes thee to except.

If guilty dread have left thee so much strength as to take up mine honour's pawn, then stop.

By that and all the rites of knighthood else will I make good against thee, arm to arm, what I have spoke, or thou canst worse devise.

Thomas Mowbray: I take it up and by that sword I swear, which gently laid my knighthood on my shoulder.

I'll answer thee in any fair degree or chivalrous design of knightly trial; and when I mount, alive may I not light, if I be traitor or unjustly fight!

King Richard II: What doth our cousin lay to Mowbray's charge?

It must be great that can inherit us so much as of a thought of ill in him.

Henry IV: Look, what I speak, my life shall prove it true, that Mowbray hath received eight thousand nobles in name of lendings for your highness' soldiers; the which he hath detained for lewd employments, like a false traitor and injurious villain.

Besides I say and will in battle prove, or here or elsewhere to the furthest verge that ever was surveyed by English eye.

All the treasons for these eighteen years complotted and contrived in this land fetch from false Mowbray their first head and spring.

Further I say, and further will maintain upon his bad life to make all this good, that he did plot the Duke of Gloucester's death suggests his soon-believing adversaries.

Consequently, like a traitor coward sluiced out his innocent soul through streams of blood, which blood, like sacrificing Abel's cries.

Even from the tongueless caverns of the earth to me, for justice and rough chastisement by the glorious worth of my descent; this arm shall do it, or this life be spent.

King Richard II: How high a pitch his resolution soars!

Thomas of Norfolk, what say'st thou to this?

Thomas Mowbray: Oh let my sovereign turn away his face and bid his ears a little while be deaf till I have told this slander of his blood, how God and good men hate so foul a liar.

King Richard II: Mowbray, impartial are our eyes and ears, where he my brother, nay, my kingdom's heir; as he is but my father's brother's son.

Now, by my sceptre's awe, I make a vow, such neighbour nearness to our sacred blood should nothing privilege him, nor partialize the unstooping firmness of my upright soul.

He is our subject, Mowbray, so art thou; free speech and fearless I to thee allow.

Thomas Mowbray: Then, Bolingbroke, as low as to thy heart, through the false passage of thy throat, thou liest.

Three parts of that receipt I had for Calais, disbursed I duly to his highness' soldiers; the other part reserved I by consent, for that my sovereign liege was in my debt upon remainder of a dear account; since last I went to France to fetch his queen.

Now swallow down that lie for Gloucester's death, I slew him not, but to my own disgrace neglected my sworn duty in that case.

For you, my noble Lord of Lancaster, the honourable father to my foe once did I lay an ambush for your life a trespass that doth vex my grieved soul, but here I last received the sacrament.

I did confess it, and exactly begged your grace's pardon, and I hope I had it.

This is my fault, as for the rest appealed, it issues from the rancour of a villain, a recreant and most degenerate traitor which in myself I boldly will defend; and interchangeably hurl down my gage upon this overweening traitor's foot, to prove myself a loyal gentleman, even in the best blood chambered in his bosom.

In haste whereof, most heartily I pray your highness to assign our trial day.

King Richard II: Wrath-kindled gentlemen, be ruled by me, let's purge this choler without letting blood.

This we prescribe, though no physician; deep malice makes too deep incision.

Forget, forgive, conclude and be agreed.

Our doctors say this is no month to bleed.

Good uncle, let this end where it begun, we'll calm the Duke of Norfolk, you your son.

John of Gaunt: To be a make-peace shall become my age.

Throw down, my son, the Duke of Norfolk's gage.

King Richard II: And, Norfolk, throw down his.

John of Gaunt: When, Harry, when? Obedience bids I should not bid again.

King Richard II: Norfolk, throw down, we bid; there is no boot.

Thomas Mowbray: Myself I throw, dread sovereign, at thy foot.

My life thou shalt command, but not my shame.

The one my duty owes, but my fair name, despite of death that lives upon my graveto dark dishonour's use thou shalt not have.

I am disgraced, impeached and baffled here, pierced to the soul with slander's venomed spear, the which no balm can cure but his heart-blood which breathed this poison.

King Richard II: Rage must be withstood, give me his gage, lions make leopards tame.

Thomas Mowbray: Yea, but not change his spots, take but my shame, and I resign my gage.

My dear dear lord, the purest treasure mortal times afford is spotless reputation, that away,

Men are but gilded loam or painted clay.

A jewel in a ten-times-barred-up chest is a bold spirit in a loyal breast.

Mine honour is my life, both grow in one; take honour from me, and my life is done.

Then, dear my liege, mine honour let me try, in that I live and for that will I die.

King Richard II: Cousin, throw up your gage, do you begin.

Henry IV: Oh God defend my soul from such deep sin!

Shall I seem crest-fallen in my father's sight?

Or with pale beggar-fear impeach my height before this out-dared dastard?

Here my tongue shall wound my honour with such feeble wrong, or sound so base a speech, my teeth shall tear the slavish motive of recanting fear, and spit it bleeding in his high disgrace where shame doth harbour, even in Mowbray's face.

(John of Gaunt exists)

King Richard II: We were not born to sue, but to command, which since we cannot do to make you friends.

Be ready, as your lives shall answer it, at Coventry, upon Saint Lambert's day; there shall your swords and lances arbitrate the swelling difference of your settled hate.

Since we can not atone you, we shall see justice design the victor's chivalry.

Lord marshal, command our officers at arms, be ready to direct these home alarms.

(Exeunt)

Act I, Scene 2

The Duke of Lancaster's palace.

(John of Gaunt with Duchess enter)

John of Gaunt: Alas, the part I had in Woodstock's blood doth more solicit me than your exclaims, to stir against the butchers of his life!

But since correction lieth in those hands, which made the fault that we cannot correct, put we our quarrel to the will of heaven who, when they see the hours ripe on earth, will rain hot vengeance on offenders' heads.

Duchess of Gloucester: Finds brotherhood in thee no sharper spur?

Hath love in thy old blood no living fire?

Edward's seven sons, whereof thyself art one, were as seven vials of his sacred blood, or seven fair branches springing from one root.

Some of those seven are dried by nature's course, some of those branches by the Destinies cut, but Thomas, my dear lord, my life, my Gloucester, one vial full of Edward's sacred blood, one flourishing branch of his most royal root, is cracked, and all the precious liquor spilt is hacked down, and his summer leaves all faded; by envy's hand and murder's bloody axe.

Ah, Gaunt, his blood was thine! that bed, that womb; that metal, that self-mould, that fashioned thee, made him a man and though thou livest and breathest.

Yet art thou slain in him, thou dost consent in some large measure to thy father's death, in that thou seest thy wretched brother die who was the model of thy father's life.

Call it not patience, Gaunt, it is despair; in suffering thus thy brother to be slaughtered.

Thou showest the naked pathway to thy life, teaching stern murder how to butcher thee that which in mean men we in title patience, is pale cold cowardice in noble breasts.

What shall I say? To safeguard thine own life, the best way is to venge my Gloucester's death.

John of Gaunt: God's is the quarrel; for God's substitute, his deputy anointed in his sight hath caused his death, the which if wrongfully, let heaven revenge, for I may never lift an angry arm against his minister.

Duchess of Gloucester: Where then, alas, may I complain myself?

John of Gaunt: To God, the widow's champion and defence.

Duchess of Gloucester: Why, then, I will.

Farewell, old Gaunt, thou goest to Coventry, there to behold our cousin Hereford and fell Mowbray fight.

Oh sit my husband's wrongs on Hereford's spear, that it may enter butcher Mowbray's breast! Or, if misfortune miss the first career, be Mowbray's sins so heavy in his bosom, they may break his foaming courser's back and throw the rider headlong in the lists, a caitiff recreant to my cousin Hereford!

Farewell, old Gaunt.

Thy sometimes brother's wife with her companion grief must end her life.

John of Gaunt: Farewell Sister.

I must to Coventry, as much good stay with thee as go with me!

Duchess of Gloucester: Yet one word more, grief boundeth where it falls, not with the empty hollowness, but weight.

I take my leave before I have begun, for sorrow ends not when it seemeth done.

Commend me to thy brother, Edmund York.

Lord, this is all; nay, yet depart not so.

Though this be all, do not so quickly go; I shall remember more.

Bid him, ah what? With all good speed at Plashy visit me.

Alack, and what shall good old York there see but empty lodgings and unfurnished walls, unpeopled offices, untrodden stones?

What hear there for welcome but my groans?

Therefore commend me, let him not come there to seek out sorrow that dwells everywhere; desolate, desolate, will I hence and die.

The last leave of thee takes my weeping eye.

(Exeunt)

Act I, Scene 3

The lists at Coventry.

(The Lord Marshal and the Duke of Aumerle enter)

Lord Marshal: My Lord Aumerle, is Harry Hereford armed?

Duke of Aumerle: Yea, at all points; and longs to enter in.

Lord Marshal: The Duke of Norfolk, sprightfully and bold, stays but the summons of the appellant's trumpet.

Duke of Aumerle: Why, then, the champions are prepared, and stay for nothing but his majesty's approach.

(The trumpets sound, and King Richard enters with his nobles, John of Gaunt, Bushy, Bagot, Green, and others; when they are set, Thomas Mowbray enters with arms as defendant, with Herald)

King Richard II: Marshal, demand of yonder champion, the cause of his arrival here in arms.

Ask him his name and orderly proceed to swear him in the justice of his cause.

Lord Marshal: In God's name and the king's, say who thou art, and why thou comest thus knightly clad in arms against what man thou comest, and what thy quarrel.

Speak truly, on thy knighthood and thy oath, as so defend thee heaven and thy valour!

Thomas Mowbray: My name is Thomas Mowbray, Duke of Norfolk, who hither come engaged by my oath; which God defend a knight should violate!

Both to defend my loyalty and truth to God, my king and my succeeding issue against the Duke of Hereford that appeals me; and by the grace of God and this mine arm to prove him, in defending of myself a traitor to my God, my king, and me.

As I truly fight, defend me heaven!

(The trumpets sound. Enter Henry Bolingbroke, appellant, in armour, with a Herald)

King Richard II: Marshal, ask yonder knight in arms, both who he is and why he cometh hither; thus plated in habiliments of war and formally according to our law, depose him in the justice of his cause.

Lord Marshal: What is thy name? And wherefore comest thou hither, before King Richard in his royal lists?

Against whom comest thou? What's thy quarrel?

Speak like a true knight, so defend thee heaven!

Henry IV: Harry of Hereford, Lancaster and Derby am I, who ready here do stand in arms to prove by God's grace and my body's valour.

In lists, on Thomas Mowbray, Duke of Norfolk, that he is a traitor, foul and dangerous to God of heaven, King Richard and to me; as I truly fight, defend me heaven!

Lord Marshal: On pain of death, no person be so bold or daring-hardy as to touch the lists, except the marshal and such officers appointed to direct these fair designs.

Henry IV: Lord marshal, let me kiss my sovereign's hand and bow my knee before his majesty.

For Mowbray and myself are like two men that vow a long and weary pilgrimage, then let us take a ceremonious leave, and loving farewell of our several friends.

Lord Marshal: The appellant in all duty greets your highness and craves to kiss your hand and take his leave.

King Richard II: We will descend and fold him in our arms.

Cousin of Hereford, as thy cause is right, so be thy fortune in this royal fight!

Farewell, my blood, which if to-day thou shed, Lament we may but revenge not thee dead.

Henry IV: Oh let no noble eye profane a tear for me, if I be gored with Mowbray's spear as confident as is the falcon's flight; against a bird do I with Mowbray fight.

My loving lord, I take my leave of you, of you my noble cousin Lord Aumerle.

Not sick, although I have to do with death, but lusty young, and cheerly drawing breath.

Lord, as at English feasts, so I regret the daintiest last to make the end most sweet.

Oh thou, the earthly author of my blood whose youthful spirit in me regenerate, doth with a twofold vigour lift me up to reach at victory above my head, add proof onto mine armour with thy prayers.

With thy blessings steel my lance's point, that it may enter Mowbray's waxen coat, and furbish new the name of John a Gaunt, even in the lusty behavior of his son.

John of Gaunt: God in thy good cause make thee prosperous!

Be swift like lightning in the execution, and let thy blows, doubly redoubled.

Fall like amazing thunder on the casque of thy adverse pernicious enemy, rouse up thy youthful blood, be valiant and live.

Henry IV: Mine innocency and Saint George to thrive!

Thomas Mowbray: However God or fortune cast my lot, there lives or dies true to King Richard's throne, a loyal, just and upright gentleman.

Never did captive with a freer heart cast off his chains of bondage and embrace, his golden uncontrolled enfranchisement, more than my dancing soul doth celebrate this feast of battle with mine adversary.

Most mighty liege, and my companion peers, take from my mouth the wish of happy years.

As gentle and as jocund as to jest go I to fight, truth hath a quiet breast.

King Richard II: Farewell, my lord: securely I espy virtue with valour couched in thine eye.

Order the trial, marshal, and begin.

Lord Marshal: Harry of Hereford, Lancaster, and Derby receive thy lance and God defend the right!

Henry IV: Strong as a tower in hope, I cry amen.

Lord Marshal: Go bear this lance to Thomas, Duke of Norfolk.

First Herald: Harry of Hereford, Lancaster and Derby stands here for God, his sovereign and himself on pain to be found false and recreant to prove the Duke of Norfolk, Thomas Mowbray, is A traitor to his God, his king, and him; and dares him to set forward to the fight.

Second Herald: Here standeth Thomas Mowbray, Duke of Norfolk, on pain to be found false and recreant both to defend himself and to approve Henry of Hereford, Lancaster, and Derby; to God, his sovereign and to him disloyal courageously and with a free desire attending but the signal to begin.

Lord Marshal: Sound trumpets and set forward, combatants.

(A charge sounded)

Stay, the king hath thrown his warder down.

King Richard II: Let them lay by their helmets and their spears and both return back to their chairs again.

Withdraw with us and let the trumpets sound while we return these dukes what we decree.

(A long flourish)

Draw near and list what with our council we have done.

For that our kingdom's earth should not be soiled with that dear blood which it hath fostered; and for our eyes do hate the dire aspect of civil wounds ploughed up with neighbours' sword.

For we think the eagle-winged pride of sky-aspiring and ambitious thoughts, with rival-hating envy, set on you to wake our peace, which in our country's cradle draws the sweet infant breath of gentle sleep; which so roused up with boisterous untuned drums with harsh resounding trumpets' dreadful bray.

Grating shock of wrathful iron arms might from our quiet confines fright fair peace and make us wade even in our kindred's blood, therefore, we banish you our territories.

You, cousin Hereford, upon pain of life, till twice five summers have enriched our fields shall not regret our fair dominions, but tread the stranger paths of banishment.

Henry IV: Your will be done: this must my comfort be, Sun that warms you here shall shine on me, and those his golden beams to you here lent shall point on me and gild my banishment.

King Richard II: Norfolk, for thee remains a heavier doom, which I with some unwillingness pronounce.

The sly slow hours shall not determinate the dateless limit of thy dear exile, the hopeless word of 'never to return' breathe I against thee, upon pain of life.

Thomas Mowbray: A heavy sentence, my most sovereign liege, and all unlooked for from your highness' mouth.

A dearer merit, not so deep a maim as to be cast forth in the common air, have I deserved at your highness' hands.

The language I have learned these forty years, my native English now I must forego, and now my tongue's use is to me no more than an unstrung viol or a harp, or like a cunning instrument cased up, or being open, put into his hands that knows no touch to tune the harmony.

Within my mouth you have engulfed my tongue, doubly portcullis'd with my teeth and lips, and dull unfeeling barren ignorance is made my gaoler to attend on me.

I am too old to fawn upon a nurse, too far in years to be a pupil now.

What is thy sentence then but speechless death, which robs my tongue from breathing native breath?

King Richard II: It boots thee not to be compassionate after our sentence plaining comes too late.

Thomas Mowbray: Then thus I turn me from my country's light, to dwell in solemn shades of endless night.

King Richard II: Return again, and take an oath with thee.

Lay on our royal sword your banished hands, swear by the duty that you owe to God our part therein we banish with yourselves to keep the oath that we administer.

You never shall, so help you truth and God!

Embrace each other's love in banishment,

Nor never look upon each other's face, nor never write, regret, nor reconcile this louring tempest of your home-bred hate; nor never by advised purpose meet to plot, contrive, or complot any ill against us, our state, our subjects, or our land.

Henry IV: I swear.

Thomas Mowbray: And I, to keep all this.

Henry IV: Norfolk, so far as to mine enemy.

By this time, had the king permitted us, one of our souls had wandered in the air.

Banishd this frail sepulchre of our flesh, as now our flesh is banished from this land, confess thy treasons were thou fly the realm; since thou hast far to go, bear not along the clogging burthen of a guilty soul.

Thomas Mowbray: No, Bolingbroke: if ever I were traitor, my name be blotted from the book of life, and I from heaven banished as from hence!

But what thou art, God, thou, and I do know, and all too soon, I fear the king shall rue.

Farewell, my liege. Now no way can I stray, save back to England, all the world's my way.

(Exits)

King Richard II: Uncle, even in the glasses of thine eyes, I see thy grieved heart; thy sad aspect hath from the number of his banished years plucked four away.

(To Henry Bolingbroke)

Six frozen winter spent, return with welcome home from banishment.

Henry IV: How long a time lies in one little word!

Four lagging winters and four wanton springs end in a word, such is the breath of kings.

John of Gaunt: I thank my liege, that in regard of me he shortens four years of my son's exile, but little vantage shall I reap thereby; for here the six years that he hath to spend can change their moons and bring their times about.

My oil-dried lamp and time-bewasted light shall be extinct with age and endless night, my inch of taper will be burnt and done, and blindfold death not let me see my son.

King Richard II: Why uncle, thou hast many years to live.

John of Gaunt: But not a minute, king, that thou canst give, shorten my days thou canst with sullen sorrow, and pluck nights from me but not lend a morrow.

Thou canst help time to furrow me with age, but stop no wrinkle in his pilgrimage, thy word is current with him for my death, but dead thy kingdom cannot buy my breath.

King Richard II: Thy son is banished upon good advice, whereto thy tongue a party-verdict gave.

Why at our justice seem'st thou then to lour?

John of Gaunt: Things sweet to taste prove in digestion sour.

You urged me as a judge, but I had rather you would have bid me argue like a father.

Oh had it been a stranger, not my child, to smooth his fault I should have been more mild.

A partial slander sought I to avoid, and in the sentence my own life destroyed.

Alas, I looked when some of you should say I was too strict to make mine own away, but you gave leave to my unwilling tongue against my will to do myself this wrong.

King Richard II: Cousin farewell, and uncle bid him so; six years we banish him, and he shall go.

(Flourish. Exeunt King Richard II and entourage)

Duke of Aumerle: Cousin, farewell: what presence must not know from where you do remain let paper show.

Lord Marshal: My lord, no leave take I, for I will ride as far as land will let me; by your side.

John of Gaunt: Oh to what purpose dost thou hoard thy words, that thou return'st no greeting to thy friends?

Henry IV: I have too few to take my leave of you when the tongue's office should be prodigal to breathe the abundant dolour of the heart.

John of Gaunt: Thy grief is but thy absence for a time.

Henry IV: Joy absent, grief is present for that time.

John of Gaunt: What is six winters? They are quickly gone.

Henry IV: To men in joy; but grief makes one hour ten.

John of Gaunt: Call it a travel that thou takest for pleasure.

Henry IV: My heart will sigh when I miscall it so, which finds it an enforced pilgrimage.

John of Gaunt: The sullen passage of thy weary steps esteem as foil wherein thou art to set the precious jewel of thy home return.

Henry IV: Nay, rather, every tedious stride I make will but remember me what a deal of world; I wander from the jewels that I love.

Must I not serve a long apprenticehood to foreign passages, and in the end having my freedom boast of nothing else but that I was a journeyman to grief?

John of Gaunt: All places that the eye of heaven visits are to a wise man ports and happy havens.

Teach thy necessity to reason thus, there is no virtue like necessity.

Think not the king did banish thee, but thou the king.

Woe doth the heavier sit where it perceives, it is but faintly borne.

Go, say I sent thee forth to purchase honour, and not the king exiled thee, or suppose devouring pestilence hangs in our air; and thou art flying to a fresher clime.

Look, what thy soul holds dear, imagine it to lie that way thou go'st, not whence thou comest.

Suppose the singing birds musicians, the grass whereon thou tread'st the presence strewed the flowers fair ladies, and thy steps no more than a delightful measure or a dance; for gnarling sorrow hath less power to bite the man that mocks at it and sets it light.

Henry IV: Oh who can hold a fire in his hand by thinking on the frosty Caucasus?

Or cloy the hungry edge of appetite by bare imagination of a feast?

Or wallow naked in December snow by thinking on fantastic summer's heat?

Oh no! The apprehension of the good gives but the greater feeling to the worse.

Fell sorrow's tooth doth never rankle more than when he bites, but lanceth not the sore.

John of Gaunt: Come, come, my son, I'll bring thee on thy way had I thy youth and cause, I would not stay.

Henry IV: Then, England's ground, farewell.

Sweet soil, adieu; my mother and my nurse, that bears me yet!

Wherever I wander, boast of this I can, though banished yet a trueborn Englishman.

(Exeunt)

Act I, Scene 4

The court.

(King Richard II enters with Bagot and Green at one door; and the Duke of Aumerle at another)

King Richard II: We did observe. Cousin Aumerle, how far brought you high Hereford on his way?

Duke of Aumerle: I brought high Hereford, if you call him so, but to the next highway, and there I left him.

King Richard II: And say, what store of parting tears were shed?

Duke of Aumerle: Faith, none for me; except the north-east wind, which then blew bitterly against our faces; awaked the sleeping rheum and so by chance did grace our hollow parting with a tear.

King Richard II: What said our cousin when you parted with him?

Duke of Aumerle: Farewell.

For my heart disdained that my tongue should so profane the word, that taught me craft to counterfeit oppression of such grief that words seemed buried in my sorrow's grave.

Marry, would the word farewell have lengthened hours and added years to his short banishment; he should have had a volume of farewells, but since it would not, he had none of me.

King Richard II: He is our cousin, cousin; but it is doubt when time shall to call him home from banishment, whether our kinsman will come to see his friends.

Ourself and Bushy, Bagot here and Green observed his courtship to the common people; how he did seem to dive into their hearts with humble and familiar courtesy; what reverence he did throw away on slaves, wooing poor craftsmen with the craft of smiles and patient underbearing of his fortune, as it were, to banish their affects with him.

Off goes his bonnet to an oyster-wench, a brace of draymen bid God speed him well, and had the tribute of his supple knee with thanks, my countrymen, my loving friends; as were our England in reversion his, and he our subjects' next degree in hope.

Green: Well, he is gone and with him go these thoughts.

Now for the rebels which stand out in Ireland, expedient manage must be made, my liege, were further leisure yield them further means for their advantage and your highness' loss.

King Richard II: We will ourself in person to this war, and for our coffers, with too great a court and liberal largess, are grown somewhat light.

We are inforced to farm our royal realm the revenue whereof shall furnish us for our affairs in hand, if that come short our substitutes at home shall have blank charters.

Whereto, when they shall know what men are rich, they shall subscribe them for large sums of gold and send them after to supply our wants; for we will make for Ireland presently.

(Bushy enters)

Bushy, what news?

Bushy: Old John of Gaunt is grievous sick, my lord, suddenly taken; and hath sent post haste to entreat your majesty to visit him.

King Richard II: Where lies he?

Bushy: At Ely House.

King Richard II: Now put it, God, in the physician's mind to help him to his grave immediately!

The lining of his coffers shall make coats to deck our soldiers for these Irish wars.

Come, gentlemen, let's all go visit him.

Pray God we may make haste, and come too late!

All: Amen.

(Exeunt)

Act II, Scene 1

Ely House.

(John of Gaunt is sick and enters with the Duke of York)

John of Gaunt: Will the king come, that I may breathe my last in wholesome counsel to his unstaid youth?

Edmund of Langley: Vex not yourself, nor strive not with your breath; for all in vain comes counsel to his ear.

John of Gaunt: Oh but they say the tongues of dying men, enforce attention like deep harmony where words are scarce, they are seldom spent in vain, for they breathe truth that breathe their words in pain.

He that no more must say is listened more than they whom youth and ease have taught to gloss; more are men's ends marked than their lives before.

The setting sun, and music at the close, as the last taste of sweets, is sweetest last, write in remembrance more than things long past.

Though Richard my life's counsel would not hear, my death's sad tale may yet undeaf his ear.

Edmund of Langley: No; it is stopped with other flattering sounds, as praises, of whose taste the wise are fond.

Lascivious metres, to whose venom sound the open ear of youth doth always listen; report of fashions in proud Italy, whose manners still our tardy apish nation limps after in base imitation.

Where doth the world thrust forth a vanity, so it be new, there's no respect how vile that is not quickly buzzed into his ears? Then all too late comes counsel to be heard, where will doth mutiny with wit's regard.

Direct not him whose way himself will choose, it is breath thou lack'st and that breath wilt thou lose.

John of Gaunt: Methinks I am a prophet new inspired, and thus expiring do foretell of him his rash fierce blaze of riot cannot last, for violent fires soon burn out themselves.

Small showers last long, but sudden storms are short, he tires betimes that spurs too fast betimes with eager feeding food doth choke the feeder.

Light vanity, insatiate cormorant, consuming means, soon preys upon itself.

This royal throne of kings, this sceptered isle, this earth of majesty, this seat of Mars, this other Eden, demi-paradise, this fortress built by Nature for herself against infection and the hand of war.

This happy breed of men, this little world, this precious stone set in the silver sea which serves it in the office of a wall, or as a moat defensive to a house, against the envy of less happier lands.

This blessed plot, this earth, this realm, this England, this nurse, this teeming womb of royal kings feared by their breed and famous by their birth, renowned for their deeds as far from home for Christian service and true chivalry.

As is the sepulchre in stubborn Jewry, of the world's ransom, blessed Mary's Son, this land of such dear souls, this dear dear land, dear for her reputation through the world is now leased out; I die pronouncing it, like to a tenement or pelting farm.

England, bound in with the triumphant sea whose rocky shore beats back the envious siege of watery Neptune, is now bound in with shame, with inky blots and rotten parchment bonds.

That England, that was wont to conquer others, hath made a shameful conquest of itself, ah, would the scandal vanish with my life, how happy then were my ensuing death!

(King Richard II and Queen, Duke of Aumerle, Bushy, Green, Bagot, Lord Ross, and Lord Willoughby enter)

Edmund of Langley: The king is come: deal mildly with his youth, for young hot colts being raged do rage the more.

Queen: How fares our noble uncle, Lancaster?

King Richard II: What comfort, man? How is it with aged Gaunt?

John of Gaunt: Oh how that name befits my composition! Old Gaunt indeed, and gaunt in being old.

Within me grief hath kept a tedious fast, and who abstains from meat that is not gaunt?

For sleeping England long time have I watched, watching breeds leanness, leanness is all gaunt.

The pleasure that some fathers feed upon is my strict fast, I mean my children's looks and therein fasting, hast thou made me gaunt.

Gaunt am I for the grave, gaunt as a grave, whose hollow womb inherits nought but bones.

King Richard II: Can sick men play so nicely with their names?

John of Gaunt: No, misery makes sport to mock itself, since thou dost seek to kill my name in me, I mock my name, great king, to flatter thee.

King Richard II: Should dying men flatter with those that live?

John of Gaunt: No, no, men living flatter those that die.

King Richard II: Thou, now a-dying, say'st thou flatterest me.

John of Gaunt: Oh no! thou diest, though I the sicker be.

King Richard II: I am in health, I breathe, and see thee ill.

John of Gaunt: Now He that made me knows I see thee ill, Ill in myself to see, and in thee seeing ill thy death-bed is no lesser than thy land

Thou liest in reputation sick, and thou are too careless patient as thou art, commit'st thy anointed body to the cure of those physicians that first wounded thee.

A thousand flatterers sit within thy crown whose compass is no bigger than thy head, and yet incaged in so small a verge; the waste is no whit lesser than thy land.

Oh had thy grandsire with a prophet's eye seen how his son's son should destroy his sons, from forth thy reach he would have laid thy shame; deposing thee before thou wert possessed, which art possessed now to depose thyself.

Why, cousin, wert thou regent of the world, it were a shame to let this land by lease; but for thy world enjoying but this land, is it not more than shame to shame it so?

Landlord of England art thou not now king.

Thy state of law is bondslave to the law; And thou—

King Richard II: A lunatic lean-witted fool, presuming on an ague's privilege, darest with thy frozen admonition make pale our cheek, chasing the royal blood with fury from his native residence.

Now, by my seat's right royal majesty, wert thou not brother to great Edward's son, this tongue that runs so roundly in thy head should run thy head from thy unreverent shoulders.

John of Gaunt: Oh spare me not, my brother Edward's son, for that I was his father Edward's son that blood already, like the pelican, hast thou tapped out and drunkenly caroused.

My brother Gloucester is a plain well-meaning soul, whom fair befall in heaven amongst happy souls!

May be a precedent and witness good that thou respect'st not spilling Edward's blood.

Join with the present sickness that I have, and thy unkindness be like crooked age, to crop at once a too long withered flower.

Live in thy shame, but die not shame with thee!

These words hereafter thy tormentors be! Convey me to my bed, then to my grave.

Love they to live that love and honour have.

(Borne off by his Attendants exists)

King Richard II: And let them die that age and sullens have for both hast thou, and both become the grave.

Edmund of Langley: I do beseech your majesty, impute his words to wayward sickliness and age in him.

He loves you, on my life, and holds you dear as Harry Duke of Hereford were he here.

King Richard II: Right, you say true, as Hereford's love, so his as theirs; so mine and all be as it is.

(Northumberland enter)

Earl of Northumberland: My liege, old Gaunt commends him to your majesty.

King Richard II: What says he? Earl of Northumberland.

Nay, nothing, all is said his tongue is now a stringless instrument.

Words, life and all, old Lancaster hath spent.

Edmund of Langley: Be York the next that must be bankrupt so!

Though death be poor, it ends a mortal woe.

King Richard II: The ripest fruit first falls, and so doth he, his time is spent; our pilgrimage must be, so much for that, now for our Irish wars

We must supplant those rough rug-headed kerns, which live like venom where no venom else, but only they have privilege to live and for these great affairs do ask some charge.

Towards our assistance we do seize to us the plate, corn, revenues and moveables,

Whereof our uncle Gaunt did stand possessed.

Edmund of Langley: How long shall I be patient? Ah, how long shall tender duty make me suffer wrong?

Not Gloucester's death, nor Hereford's banishment.

Not Gaunt's rebukes, nor England's private wrongs, nor the prevention of poor Bolingbroke about his marriage; nor my own disgrace, have ever made me sour my patient cheek, or bend one wrinkle on my sovereign's face.

I am the last of noble Edward's sons of whom thy father, Prince of Wales was first in war was never lion raged more fierce; in peace was never gentle lamb more mild, than was that young and princely gentleman.

His face thou hast, for even so looked he, accomplished with the number of thy hours, but when he frowned, it was against the French and not against his friends; his noble hand did will what he did spend and spent not that which his triumphant father's hand had won.

His hands were guilty of no kindred blood, but bloody with the enemies of his kin.

Oh Richard! York is too far gone with grief, or else he never would compare between.

King Richard II: Why, uncle, what's the matter?

Edmund of Langley: Oh my liege, pardon me, if you please, if not I am pleased not to be pardoned, am content with all.

Seek you to seize and gripe into your hands the royalties and rights of banished Hereford?

Is not Gaunt dead, and doth not Hereford live?

Was not Gaunt just, and is not Harry true?

Did not the one deserve to have an heir?

Is not his heir a well-deserving son?

Take Hereford's rights away, and take from time his charters and his customary rights; let not to-morrow then ensue to-day.

Be not thyself, for how art thou a king, but by fair sequence and succession?

Now, afore God, God forbid I say true!

If you do wrongfully seize Hereford's rights, call in the letters patent that he hath by his attorneys-general to sue his livery, and deny his offered homage.

You pluck a thousand dangers on your head, you lose a thousand well-disposed hearts and prick my tender patience, to those thoughts which honour and allegiance cannot think.

King Richard II: Think what you will, we seize into our hands his plate, his goods, his money and his lands.

Edmund of Langley: I'll not be by the while, my liege, farewell.

What will ensue hereof, there's none can tell, but by bad courses may be understood that their events can never fall out good.

(Exits)

King Richard II: Go, Bushy, to the Earl of Wiltshire straight, bid him repair to us to Ely House to see this business.

To-morrow next we will for Ireland, and it is time; I throw and we create, in absence of ourself, our uncle York lord governor of England; for he is just and always loved us well.

Come on, our queen: to-morrow must we part, be merry, for our time of stay is short

(Flourishing)

(Exeunt King Richard II, Queen, Duke of Aumerle, Bushy, Green, and Bagot)

Earl of Northumberland, well lords, the Duke of Lancaster is dead.

Lord Ross: And living too; for now his son is duke.

Lord Willoughby: Barely in title, not in revenue.

Earl of Northumberland: Richly in both, if justice had her right.

Lord Ross: My heart is great; but it must break with silence,

Here it be disburdened with a liberal tongue.

Earl of Northumberland: Nay, speak thy mind; and let him never speak more

That speaks thy words again to do thee harm!

Lord Willoughby: Tends that thou wouldst speak to the Duke of Hereford?

If it be so, out with it boldly, man.

Quick is mine ear to hear of good towards him.

Lord Ross: No good at all that I can do for him, unless you call it good to pity him, bereft and gelded of his patrimony.

Earl of Northumberland: Now, before God, it is shame such wrongs are borne in him, a royal prince, and many more of noble blood in this declining land.

The king is not himself, but basely led by flatterers, and what they will inform merely in hate against any of us all, that will the king severely prosecute against us, our lives, our children, and our heirs.

Lord Ross: The commons hath he pilled with grievous taxes, and quite lost their hearts.

The nobles hath he fined for ancient quarrels, and quite lost their hearts.

Lord Willoughby: And daily new exactions are devised, as blanks, benevolences, and I know not what, but what, of God's name doth become of this?

Earl of Northumberland: Wars have not wasted it, for warred he hath not, but basely yielded upon compromise that which his noble ancestors achieved with blows; more hath he spent in peace than they in wars.

Lord Ross: The Earl of Wiltshire hath the realm in farm.

Lord Willoughby: The king's grown bankrupt, like a broken man.

Earl of Northumberland: Reproach and dissolution hangeth over him.

Lord Ross: He hath not money for these Irish wars, his burthenous taxations notwithstanding, but by the robbing of the banished duke.

Earl of Northumberland: His noble kinsman, most degenerate king!

But, lords, we hear this fearful tempest sing, yet see no shelter to avoid the storm; we see the wind sit sore upon our sails, and yet we strike not, but securely perish.

Lord Ross: We see the very wreck that we must suffer, and unavoided is the danger now

for suffering so the causes of our wreck.

Earl of Northumberland: Not so; even through the hollow eyes of death I spy life peering; but I dare not say how near the tidings of our comfort is.

Lord Willoughby: Nay, let us share thy thoughts, as thou dost ours.

Lord Ross: Be confident to speak, Northumberland.

We three are but thyself, and speaking so thy words are but as thoughts; therefore be bold.

Earl of Northumberland: Then thus: I have from Port le Blanc, a bay in Brittany received intelligence

That Harry Duke of Hereford, Rainold Lord Cobham, that late broke from the Duke of Exeter, his brother, Archbishop late of Canterbury Sir Thomas Erpingham, Sir John Ramston, Sir John Norbery, Sir Robert Waterton and Francis Quoint.

All these well furnished by the Duke of Bretagne with eight tall ships, three thousand men of war, are making hither with all due expedience and shortly mean to touch our northern shore.

Perhaps they had ere this, but that they stay the first departing of the king for Ireland.

If then we shall shake off our slavish yoke, Imp out our drooping country's broken wing, redeem from broking pawn the blemished crown, wipe off the dust that hides our sceptre's gilt and make high majesty look like itself away with me in post to Ravenspurgh.

If you faint, as fearing to do so, stay and be secret, and myself will go.

Lord Ross: To horse, to horse! Urge doubts to them that fear.

Lord Willoughby: Hold out my horse, and I will first be there.

(Exeunt)

Act II, Scene 2

The palace.

(Queen, Bushy, and Bagot enter)

Bushy: Madam, your majesty is too much sad:

You promised, when you parted with the king to lay aside life-harming heaviness and entertain a cheerful disposition.

Queen: To please the king I did; to please myself I cannot do it, yet I know no cause why I should welcome such a guest as grief, save bidding farewell to so sweet a guest as my sweet Richard.

Yet again, methinks some unborn sorrow, ripe in fortune's womb, is coming towards me and my inward soul with nothing trembles.

At something it grieves, more than with parting from my lord the king.

Bushy: Each substance of a grief hath twenty shadows, which shows like grief itself, but is not so for sorrow's eye, glazed with blinding tears divides one thing entire to many objects; like perspectives which rightly gazed upon show nothing but confusion, eyed awry distinguish form.

So your sweet majesty, looking awry upon your lord's departure, find shapes of grief more than himself, to wail; which looked on as it is, is nought but shadows of what it is not.

Then, thrice-gracious queen, more than your lord's departure weep not: more's not seen; or if it be, it is with false sorrow's eye, which for things true weeps things imaginary.

Queen: It may be so; but yet my inward soul persuades me it is otherwise, however it be, I cannot but be sad; so heavy sad as though on thinking, thinking on no thought I think, makes me with heavy nothing faint and shrink.

Bushy: It is nothing but conceit, my gracious Lady.

Queen: It is nothing less, conceit is still derived from some forefather grief, mine is not so for nothing had begot my something grief; or something hath the nothing that I grieve.

It is in reversion that I do possess, but what it is, that is not yet known; what I cannot name, it is nameless woe, I know it.

(Green enters)

Green: God save your majesty! And well met, gentlemen.

I hope the king is not yet shipped for Ireland.

Queen: Why hopest thou so? It is better hope he is, for his designs crave haste, his haste good hope.

Then wherefore dost thou hope he is not shipped?

Green: That he, our hope, might have retired his power and driven into despair an enemy's hope; who strongly hath set footing in this land.

The banished Bolingbroke repeals himself, and with uplifted arms is safe arrived at Ravenspurgh.

Queen: Now God in heaven forbid!

Green: Ah, madam, it is too true, and know that it is worse, for the Lord Northumberland, his son young Henry Percyr, the Lords of Ross, Beaumond, and Willoughby, with all their powerful friends, are fled to him.

Bushy: Why have you not proclaimed Northumberland and all the rest revolted faction traitors?

Green: We have: whereupon the Earl of Worcester hath broke his staff, resigned his stewardship, and all the household servants fled with him to Bolingbroke.

Queen: So, Green, thou art the midwife to my woe, and Bolingbroke my sorrow's dismal heir.

Now hath my soul brought forth her prodigy, and I, a gasping new-delivered mother, have woe to woe, sorrow to sorrow joined.

Bushy: Despair not, madam.

Queen: Who shall hinder me?

I will despair, and be at enmity with cozening hope.

He is a flatterer, a parasite, a keeper back of death who gently would dissolve the bands of life; which false hope lingers in extremity.

(Duke of York enters)

Green: Here comes the Duke of York.

Queen: With signs of war about his aged neck.

Oh full of careful business are his looks!

Uncle, for God's sake, speak comfortable words.

Edmund of Langley: Should I do so, I should belie my thoughts.

Comfort's in heaven; and we are on the earth, where nothing lives but crosses, cares and grief.

Your husband, he is gone to save far off, whilst others come to make him lose at home.

Here am I left to underprop his land who, weak with age, cannot support myself.

Now comes the sick hour that his surfeit made, now shall he try his friends that flattered him.

(A Servant enters)

Servant: My lord, your son was gone before I came.

Edmund of Langley: He was? Why, so! go all which way it will!

The nobles they are fled, the commons they are cold, and will, I fear, revolt on Hereford's side.

Sirrah, get thee to Plashy, to my sister Gloucester; bid her send me presently a thousand pound.

Hold, take my ring.

Servant: My lord, I had forgot to tell your lordship to-day, as I came by, I called there; but I shall grieve you to report the rest.

Edmund of Langley: What is it, knave?

Servant: An hour before I came, the Duchess died.

Edmund of Langley: God for his mercy! What a tide of woes comes rushing on this woeful land at once!

I know not what to do, I would to God, so my untruth had not provoked him to it, the king had cut off my head with my brother's.

What, are there no posts dispatched for Ireland?

How shall we do for money for these wars?

Come, sister, cousin, I would say, pray, pardon me.

Go, fellow, get thee home, provide some carts and bring away the armour that is there.

(Servant exits)

Gentlemen, will you go muster men?

If I know how or which way to order these affairs thus thrust disorderly into my hands, never believe me; both are my kinsmen:

The one is my sovereign, whom both my oath and duty bids defend; the other again is my kinsman, whom the king hath wronged, whom conscience and my kindred bids to right.

Well, somewhat we must do, come, cousin, I'll dispose of you.

Gentlemen, go, muster up your men, and meet me presently at Berkeley.

I should to Plashy too, but time will not permit.

All is uneven, and everything is left at six and seven.

(Exeunt Duke of York and Queen)

Bushy: The wind sits fair for news to go to Ireland, but none returns.

For us to levy power proportionable to the enemy is all impossible.

Green: Besides, our nearness to the king in love is near the hate of those love not the king.

Bagot: And that's the wavering commons, for their love Lies in their purses, and whoso empties them by so much fills their hearts with deadly hate.

Bushy: Wherein the king stands generally condemned.

Bagot: If judgement lie in them, then so do we, because we ever have been near the king.

Green: Well, I will for refuge straight to Bristol castle.

The Earl of Wiltshire is already there.

Bushy: Thither will I with you, for little office the hateful commons will perform for us, except like curs to tear us all to pieces.

Will you go along with us?

Bagot: No; I will to Ireland to his majesty.

Farewell.

If heart's presages be not vain, we three here art that ne'er shall meet again.

Bushy: That's as York thrives to beat back Bolingbroke.

Green: Alas, poor duke! The task he undertakes is numbering sands and drinking oceans dry; where one on his side fights, thousands will fly.

Farewell at once, for once, for all, and ever.

Bushy: Well, we may meet again.

Bagot: I fear me, never.

(Exeunt)

Act II, Scene 3

Wilds in Gloucestershire.

(Henry Bolingbroke and Northumberland enter with Forces)

Henry IV: How far is it, my lord, to Berkeley now?

Earl of Northumberland: Believe me, noble lord, I am a stranger here in Gloucestershire.

These high wild hills and rough uneven ways draws out our miles, and makes them wearisome, and yet your fair discourse hath been as sugar, making the hard way sweet and delectable; but I bethink me what a weary way from Ravenspurgh to Cotswold will be found in Ross and Willoughby wanting your company.

Which I protest, hath very much beguiled the tediousness and process of my travel, but theirs is sweetened with the hope to have the present benefit which I possess; and hope to joy is little less in joy than hope enjoyed.

By this the weary lords shall make their way seem short, as mine hath done by sight of what I have, your noble company.

Henry IV: Of much less value is my company than your good words, but who comes here?

(Henry Percyr enter)

Earl of Northumberland: It is my son, young Harry Percy, sent from my brother Worcester, whencesoever.

Harry, how fares your uncle?

Hotspur (Henry Percyr): I had thought, my lord, to have learned his health of you.

Earl of Northumberland: Why, is he not with the queen?

Hotspur (Henry Percyr): No, my good Lord; he hath forsook the court,

Broken his staff of office and dispersed the household of the king.

Earl of Northumberland: What was his reason?

He was not so resolved when last we spake together.

Hotspur (Henry Percyr): Because your lordship was proclaimed traitor.

But he, my lord, is gone to Ravenspurgh to offer service to the Duke of Hereford, and sent me over by Berkeley to discover what power the Duke of York had levied there; then with directions to repair to Ravenspurgh.

Earl of Northumberland: Have you forgot the Duke of Hereford, boy?

Hotspur (Henry Percyr): No, my good lord, for that is not forgot which never I did remember, to my knowledge I never in my life did look on him.

Earl of Northumberland: Then learn to know him now; this is the duke.

Hotspur (Henry Percyr): My gracious lord, I tender you my service such as it is, being tender, raw and young; which elder days shall ripen and confirm to more approved service and desert.

Henry IV: I thank thee, gentle Percy; and be sure I count myself in nothing else so happy as in a soul remembering my good friends, and as my fortune ripens with thy love, it shall be still thy true love's recompense.

My heart this covenant makes, my hand thus seals it.

Earl of Northumberland: How far is it to Berkeley? And what stir keeps good old York there with his men of war?

Hotspur (Henry Percyr): There stands the castle, by yon tuft of trees, manned with three hundred men, as I have heard; and in it are the Lords of York, Berkeley, and Seymour; none else of name and noble estimate.

(Lord Ross and Lord Willoughby enter)

Earl of Northumberland: Here come the Lords of Ross and Willoughby, bloody with spurring, fiery-red with haste.

Henry IV: Welcome, my lords.

I know your love pursues a banished traitor, all my treasury is yet but unfelt thanks, which more enriched shall be your love and labour's recompense.

Lord Ross: Your presence makes us rich, most noble Lord.

Lord Willoughby: And far surmounts our labour to attain it.

Henry IV: Evermore thanks, the exchequer of the poor, which till my infant fortune comes to years, stands for my bounty.

But who comes here?

(Lord Berkeley enters)

Earl of Northumberland: It is my Lord of Berkeley, as I guess.

Lord Berkeley: My Lord of Hereford, my message is to you.

Henry IV: My lord, my answer is, to Lancaster, and I am come to seek that name in England; and I must find that title in your tongue before I make reply to aught you say.

Lord Berkeley: Mistake me not, my lord; 'tis not my meaning to raze one title of your honour out.

To you my lord, I come, what lord you will from the most gracious regent of this land, the Duke of York, to know what pricks you on to take advantage of the absent time and fright our native peace with self-born arms.

(Duke of York enters attended)

Henry IV: I shall not need transport my words by you, here comes his grace in person.

My noble uncle!

(Kneels)

Edmund of Langley: Show me thy humble heart, and not thy knee, whose duty is deceivable and false.

Henry IV: My gracious uncle.

Edmund of Langley: Tut, tut!

Grace me no grace, nor uncle me no uncle.

I am no traitor's uncle, and that word grace, in an ungracious mouth is but profane.

Why have those banished and forbidden legs dared once to touch a dust of England's ground?

But then more 'why?' why have they dared to march so many miles upon her peaceful bosom, frighting her pale-faced villages with war and ostentation of despised arms?

Comest thou because the anointed king is hence?

Why, foolish boy, the king is left behind, and in my loyal bosom lies his power.

Were I but now the lord of such hot youth, as when brave Gaunt, thy father, and myself rescued the Black Prince, that young Mars of men, from forth the ranks of many thousand French.

Oh then how quickly should this arm of mine, now prisoner to the palsy, chastise thee and minister correction to thy fault!

Henry IV: My gracious uncle, let me know my fault:

On what condition stands it and wherein?

Edmund of Langley: Even in condition of the worst degree, in gross rebellion and detested treason.

Thou art a banished man, and here art come before the expiration of thy time, in braving arms against thy sovereign.

Henry IV: As I was banished, I was banished Hereford, but as I come, I come for Lancaster; and, noble uncle, I beseech your grace look on my wrongs with an indifferent eye.

You are my father, for methinks in you I see old Gaunt alive, oh then my father, will you permit that I shall stand condemned a wandering vagabond; my rights and royalties plucked from my arms perforce and given away to upstart unthrifts?

Wherefore was I born? If that my cousin king be King of England, it must be granted I am Duke of Lancaster.

You have a son, Aumerle, my noble cousin; had you first died, and he been thus trod down he should have found his uncle Gaunt a father, to rouse his wrongs and chase them to the bay.

I am denied to sue my livery here, and yet my letters-patents give me leave.

My father's goods are all distrained and sold, and these and all are all amiss employed; what would you have me do? I am a subject and I challenge law.

Attorneys are denied me, and therefore personally I lay my claim to my inheritance of free descent.

Earl of Northumberland: The noble duke hath been too much abused.

Lord Ross: It stands your grace upon to do him right.

Lord Willoughby: Base men by his endowments are made great.

Edmund of Langley: My lords of England, let me tell you this, I have had feeling of my cousin's wrongs and laboured all I could to do him right; but in this kind to come, in braving arms, be his own carver and cut out his way to find out right with wrong.

It may not be, and you that do abet him in this kind cherish rebellion and are rebels all.

Earl of Northumberland: The noble duke hath sworn his coming is, but for his own and for the right of that, we all have strongly sworn to give him aid; and let him never see joy that breaks that oath!

Edmund of Langley: Well, well, I see the issue of these arms, I cannot mend it, I must needs confess because my power is weak and all ill left.

If I could, by him that gave me life, I would attach you all and make you stoop unto the sovereign mercy of the king; but since I cannot, be it known to you I do remain as neuter.

So, fare you well, unless you please to enter in the castle, and there repose you for this night.

Henry IV: An offer uncle, that we will accept, but we must win your grace to go with us.

To Bristol castle, which they say is held by Bushy, Bagot and their complices, the caterpillars of the commonwealth; which I have sworn to weed and pluck away.

Edmund of Langley: It may be I will go with you, but yet I'll pause, for I am loath to break our country's laws.

Nor friends nor foes, to me welcome you are.

Things past redress are now with me past care.

(Exeunt)

Act II, Scene 4

A camp in Wales.

(Earl of Salisbury and a Welsh Captain enter)

Captain: My lord of Salisbury, we have stayed ten days, and hardly kept our countrymen together, and yet we hear no tidings from the king; therefore we will disperse ourselves.

Farewell.

Earl of Salisbury: Stay yet another day, thou trusty Welshman.

The king reposeth all his confidence in thee.

Captain: It is thought the king is dead, we will not stay.

The bay-trees in our country are all withered and meteors fright the fixed stars of heaven; the pale-faced moon looks bloody on the earth and lean-looked prophets whisper fearful change.

Rich men look sad and ruffians dance and leap, the one in fear to lose what they enjoy, the other to enjoy by rage and war; these signs forerun the death or fall of kings.

Farewell.

Our countrymen are gone and fled, as well assured Richard their king is dead.

(Exits)

Earl of Salisbury: Ah, Richard, with the eyes of heavy mind I see thy glory like a shooting star, fall to the base earth from the firmament.

Thy sun sets weeping in the lowly west, witnessing storms to come, woe and unrest.

Thy friends are fled to wait upon thy foes, and crossly to thy good all fortune goes.

(Exits)

Act III, Scene 1

Before the castle. (Bristol)

(Henry Bolingbroke, Duke of York, Northumberland, Lord Ross, Henry Percyr, Lord Willoughby enter with Bushy and Green, prisoners)

Henry IV: Bring forth these men.

Bushy and Green, I will not vex your souls, since presently your souls must part your bodies, with too much urging your pernicious lives for it were no charity; yet to wash your blood from off my hands, here in the view of men I will unfold some causes of your deaths.

You have misled a prince, a royal king, a happy gentleman in blood and lineaments by you unhappied and disfigured clean, you have in manner with your sinful hours made a divorce betwixt his queen and him; broke the possession of a royal bed and stained the beauty of a fair queen's cheeks with tears drawn from her eyes by your foul wrongs.

Myself, a prince by fortune of my birth, near to the king in blood, and near in love till you did make him misinterpret me have stooped my neck under your injuries and sighed my English breath in foreign clouds.

Eating the bitter bread of banishment, whilst you have fed upon my signories, disparked my parks and felled my forest woods from my own windows torn my household coat razed out my imprese, leaving me no sign; save men's opinions and my living blood to show the world I am a gentleman.

This and much more, much more than twice all this, condemns you to the death.

See them delivered over to execution and the hand of death.

Bushy: More welcome is the stroke of death to me than Bolingbroke to England.

Lords, farewell.

Green: My comfort is that heaven will take our souls and plague injustice with the pains of hell.

Henry IV: My Lord Northumberland, see them dispatched.

(Exeunt Northumberland and others, with the prisoners)

Uncle, you say the queen is at your house.

For God's sake, fairly let her be entreated, tell her I send to her my kind commends.

Take special care my greetings be delivered.

Edmund of Langley: A gentleman of mine I have dispatched with letters of your love to her at large.

Henry IV: Thank, gentle uncle. Come, lords, away to fight with Glendower and his complices.

Awhile to work, and after holiday.

(Exeunt)

Act III, Scene 2

A castle in view. (The coast of Wales)

(Drums, flourish and many colours)

(King Richard II, the Bishop of Carlisle, Duke of Aumerle, and Soldiers enter)

King Richard II: Barkloughly castle call they this at hand?

Duke of Aumerle: Yes my Lord, how brooks your grace the air, after your late tossing on the breaking seas?

King Richard II: Needs must I like it well, I weep for joy to stand upon my kingdom once again.

Dear earth, I do salute thee with my hand, though rebels wound thee with their horses' hoofs.

As a long-parted mother with her child plays fondly with her tears and smiles in meeting;

so weeping, smiling, greet I thee, my earth and do thee favours with my royal hands.

Feed not thy sovereign's foe, my gentle earth, nor with thy sweets comfort his ravenous sense; but let thy spiders, that suck up thy venom and heavy-gaited toads lie in their way; doing annoyance to the treacherous feet which with usurping steps do trample thee.

Yield stinging nettles to mine enemies, and when they from thy bosom pluck a flower, guard it, I pray thee with a lurking adder whose double tongue may with a mortal touch.

Throw death upon thy sovereign's enemies, mock not my senseless conjuration lords.

This earth shall have a feeling and these stones prove armed soldiers, here her native king shall falter under foul rebellion's arms.

Bishop of Carlisle: Fear not my lord, that Power that made you king hath power to keep you king in spite of all.

The means that heaven yields must be embraced, and not neglected; else if heaven would, and we will not, heaven's offer we refuse the proffered means of succor and redress.

Duke of Aumerle: He means, my lord, that we are too remiss, whilst Bolingbroke, through our security grows strong and great in substance and in power.

King Richard II: Discomfortable cousin! know'st thou not that when the searching eye of heaven is hid, behind the globe, that lights the lower world, then thieves and robbers range abroad unseen in murders and in outrage, boldly here.

But when from under this terrestrial ball he fires the proud tops of the eastern pines, and darts his light through every guilty hole, then murders, treasons and detested sins under the cloak of night; the cloak of night being plucked from off their backs, they stand bare and naked, trembling at themselves?

So when this thief, this traitor Bolingbroke, who all this while hath revelled in the night whilst we were wandering with the antipodes, shall see us rising in our throne, the east,

His treasons will sit blushing in his face, not able to endure the sight of day, but self-affrighted tremble at his sin.

Not all the water in the rough rude sea can wash the balm off from an anointed king; the breath of worldly men cannot depose the deputy elected by the Lord.

For every man that Bolingbroke hath pressed to lift shrewd steel against our golden crown, God for his Richard hath in heavenly pay a glorious angel.

Then, if angels fight, weak men must fall, for heaven still guards the right.

(Earl of Salisbury enters)

Welcome, my Lord: how far off lies your power?

Earl of Salisbury: Nor near nor farther off, my gracious lord, than this weak arm; discomfort guides my tongue and bids me speak of nothing but despair.

One day too late, I fear me, noble lord hath clouded all thy happy days on earth.

Oh call back yesterday, bid time return, and thou shalt have twelve thousand fighting men!

To-day, to-day, unhappy day, too late, overthrows thy joys, friends, fortune and thy state, for all the Welshmen, hearing thou wert dead.

Are gone to Bolingbroke, dispersed and fled.

Duke of Aumerle: Comfort, my liege, why looks your grace so pale?

King Richard II: But now the blood of twenty thousand men did triumph in my face, and they are fled, and till so much blood thither come again; have I not reason to look pale and dead?

All souls that will be safe fly from my side for time hath set a blot upon my pride.

Duke of Aumerle: Comfort, my liege; remember who you are.

King Richard II: I had forgot myself, am I not king?

Awake, thou coward majesty! Thou sleepest.

Is not the king's name twenty thousand names?

Arm, arm, my name! A puny subject strikes at thy great glory.

Look not to the ground, ye favourites of a king, are we not high?

High be our thoughts, I know my uncle York hath power enough to serve our turn.

But who comes here?

(Sir Stephen Scroop enters)

Sir Stephen Scroop: More health and happiness betide my liege than can my care-tuned tongue deliver him!

King Richard II: Mine ear is open and my heart prepared, the worst is worldly loss thou canst unfold.

Say, is my kingdom lost? Why, it was my care and what loss is it to be rid of care?

Strives Bolingbroke to be as great as we?

Greater he shall not be; if he serve God, we'll serve Him too and be his fellow so.

Revolt our subjects? That we cannot mend, they break their faith to God as well as us.

Cry woe, destruction, ruin and decay.

The worst is death, and death will have his day.

Sir Stephen Scroop, glad am I that your highness is so armed to bear the tidings of calamity.

Like an unseasonable stormy day, which makes the silver rivers drown their shores, as if the world were all dissolved to tears.

So high above his limits swells the rage of Bolingbroke, covering your fearful land with hard bright steel and hearts harder than steel.

White-beards have armed their thin and hairless scalps against thy majesty; boys with women's voices strive to speak big and clap their female joints in stiff unwieldy arms against thy crown.

The very beadsmen learn to bend their bows of double-fatal yew against thy state; yea, distaff-women manage rusty bills against thy seat.

Both young and old rebel, and all goes worse than I have power to tell.

King Richard II: Too well, too well thou tell'st a tale so ill.

Where is the Earl of Wiltshire? Where is Bagot?

What is become of Bushy? Where is Green?

That they have let the dangerous enemy measure our confines with such peaceful steps?

If we prevail, their heads shall pay for it, I warrant they have made peace with Bolingbroke.

Sir Stephen Scroop: Peace have they made with him indeed, my Lord.

King Richard II: Oh villains, vipers, damned without redemption!

Dogs, easily won to fawn on any man!

Snakes, in my heart-blood warmed, that sting my heart!

Three Judases, each one thrice worse than Judas!

Would they make peace? Terrible hell make war upon their spotted souls for this offence!

Sir Stephen Scroop: Sweet love, I see changing his property, turns to the sourest and most deadly hate; again uncurse their souls.

Their peace is made with heads and not with hands, those whom you curse have felt the worst of death's destroying wound and lie full low, graved in the hollow ground.

Duke of Aumerle: Is Bushy, Green, and the Earl of Wiltshire dead?

Sir Stephen Scroop: Ay, all of them at Bristol lost their heads.

Duke of Aumerle: Where is the duke my father with his power?

King Richard II: No matter where, of comfort no man speak.

Let's talk of graves, of worms, and epitaphs; make dust our paper and with rainy eyes write sorrow on the bosom of the earth, let's choose executors and talk of wills.

And yet not so, for what can we bequeath save our deposed bodies to the ground?

Our lands, our lives and all are Bolingbroke's, and nothing can we call our own but death and that small model of the barren earth which serves as paste and cover to our bones.

For God's sake, let us sit upon the ground and tell sad stories of the death of kings.

How some have been deposed, some slain in war, some haunted by the ghosts they have deposed; some poisoned by their wives, some sleeping killed, all murdered.

For within the hollow crown that rounds the mortal temples of a king, keeps Death his court and there the antic sits scoffing his state and grinning at his pomp; allowing him a breath a little.

A scene to monarchize, be feared and kill with looks, infusing him with self and vain conceit, as if this flesh which walls about our life, were brass impregnable, and humoured thus comes at the last and with a little pin bores through his castle wall, and farewell king!

Cover your heads and mock not flesh and blood with solemn reverence, throw away respect, tradition, form and ceremonious duty; for you have but mistook me all this while.

I live with bread like you, feel want, taste grief, need friends, subjected thus; how can you say to me, I am a king?

Bishop of Carlisle: My lord, wise men never sit and wail their woes, but presently prevent the ways to wail.

To fear the foe, since fear oppresseth strength, gives in your weakness strength unto your foe, and so your follies fight against yourself.

Fear and be slain, no worse can come to fight, and fight and die is death destroying death where fearing dying pays death servile breath.

Duke of Aumerle: My father hath a power; inquire of him and learn to make a body of a limb.

King Richard II: Thou chidest me well: proud Bolingbroke, I come to change blows with thee for our day of doom.

This ague fit of fear is over-blown, an easy task it is to win our own.

Say, Scroop, where lies our uncle with his power?

Speak sweetly, man, although thy looks be sour.

Sir Stephen Scroop: Men judge by the complexion of the sky the state and inclination of the day.

So may you by my dull and heavy eye, my tongue hath but a heavier tale to say.

I play the torturer, by small and small to lengthen out the worst that must be spoken.

Your uncle York is joined with Bolingbroke, and all your northern castles yielded up, and all your southern gentlemen in arms upon his party.

King Richard II: Thou hast said enough.

Beshrew thee, cousin, which didst lead me forth.

(To Duke of Aumerle)

Of that sweet way I was in to despair!

What say you now? What comfort have we now?

By heaven, I'll hate him everlastingly that bids me be of comfort any more.

Go to Flint castle: there I'll pine away a king whose slave shall kingly woe obey.

That power I have, discharge, and let them go to ear the land that hath some hope to grow, for I have none.

Let no man speak again to alter this, for counsel is but vain.

Duke of Aumerle: My liege, one word.

King Richard II: He does me double wrong that wounds me with the flatteries of his tongue.

Discharge my followers: let them hence away from Richard's night to Bolingbroke's fair day.   **(Exeunt)**

Act III, Scene 3

Before Flint castle. (Wales)

(Henry Bolingbroke, Duke of York, Northumberland, Attendants, and forces enter, with drum and colours,)

Henry IV: So that by this intelligence we learn the Welshmen are dispersed, and Salisbury is gone to meet the king, who lately landed with some few private friends upon this coast.

Earl of Northumberland: The news is very fair and good, my lord.

Richard not far from hence hath hid his head.

Edmund of Langley: It would beseem the Lord Northumberland to say King Richard alas the heavy day when such a sacred king should hide his head.

Earl of Northumberland: Your grace mistakes, only to be brief was his title left out.

Edmund of Langley: The time hath been, would you have been so brief with him, he would have been so brief with you, to shorten you, for taking so the head, your whole head's length.

Henry IV: Mistake not, uncle, further than you should.

Edmund of Langley: Take not, good cousin, further than you should.

Lest you mistake the heavens are over our heads.

Henry IV: I know it, uncle, and oppose not myself against their will.

But who comes here?

(Henry Percyr enters)

Welcome, Harry: what, will not this castle yield?

Hotspur (Henry Percyr) The castle royally is manned, my lord, against thy entrance.

Henry IV: Royally!

Why, it contains no king?

Hotspur (Henry Percyr): Yes, my good lord, it doth contain a king; King Richard lies within the limits of yon lime and stone.

And with him are the Lord Aumerle, Lord Salisbury, Sir Stephen Scroop, besides a clergyman of holy reverence; who I cannot learn of.

Earl of Northumberland: Oh belike, it is the Bishop of Carlisle.

Henry IV: Noble lords, go to the rude ribs of that ancient castle through brazen trumpet send the breath of spoken words into his ruined ears, and thus deliver.

Henry Bolingbroke, on both his knees doth kiss King Richard's hand, and sends allegiance and true faith of heart to his most royal person, hither come.

Even at his feet to lay my arms and power, provided that my banishment repealed and lands restored again be freely granted.

If not, I'll use the advantage of my power and lay the summer's dust with showers of blood rained from the wounds of slaughtered Englishmen.

The which, how far off from the mind of Bolingbroke it is, such crimson tempest should bedrench the fresh green lap of fair King Richard's land; my stooping duty tenderly shall show.

Go, signify as much, while here we marcupon the grassy carpet of this plain.

Let's march without the noise of threatening drum, that from this castle's tattered battlements.

Our fair appointments may be well perused.

Methinks King Richard and myself should meet with no less terror than the elements than of fire and water, when their thundering shock at meeting tears, the cloudy cheeks of heaven.

Be he the fire, I'll be the yielding water.

The rage be his, whilst on the earth I rain my waters; on the earth and not on him.

March on, and mark King Richard how he looks.

(Speak without words, and answer within area)

(Flourishing)

(King Richard II, the Bishop of Carlisle, Duke of Aumerle, Sir Stephen Scroop, and Earl of Salisbury enter on walls)

See, see, King Richard doth himself appear as doth the blushing discontented sun from out the fiery portal of the east; when he perceives the envious clouds are bent to dim his glory and to stain the track of his bright passage to the occident.

Edmund of Langley: Yet looks he like a king: behold, his eye as bright as is the eagle's, lightens forth controlling majesty: alas, alas, for woe, that any harm should stain so fair a show!

King Richard II: We are amazed; and thus long have we stood

To watch the fearful bending of thy knee,

(To Northumberland)

Because we thought ourself thy lawful king, and if we be, how dare thy joints forget to pay their awful duty to our presence?

If we be not, show us the hand of God that hath dismissed us from our stewardship; for well we know, no hand of blood and bone can gripe the sacred handle of our sceptre unless he do profane, steal, or usurp.

Though you think that all, as you have done, have torn their souls by turning them from us, and we are barren and bereft of friends; yet know my master, God omnipotent is mustering in his clouds on our behalf armies of pestilence.

They shall strike your children yet unborn and unbegot that lift your vassal hands against my head and threat the glory of my precious crown.

Tell Bolingbroke, for yond methinks he stands, that every stride he makes upon my land is dangerous treason; he is come to open the purple testament of bleeding war, but here the crown he looks for live in peace.

Ten thousand bloody crowns of mothers' sons shall ill become the flower of England's face, change the complexion of her maid-pale peace to scarlet indignation and bedew her pastures' grass with faithful English blood.

Earl of Northumberland: The king of heaven forbid our lord the king should so with civil and uncivil arms be rushed upon!

Thy thrice noble cousin Harry Bolingbroke doth humbly kiss thy hand, and by the honourable tomb he swears that stands upon your royal grandsire's bones, and by the royalties of both your bloods as currents that spring from one most gracious head.

By the buried hand of warlike Gaunt, and by the worth and honour of himself, comprising all that may be sworn or said his coming hither hath no further scope than for his lineal royalties and to beg enfranchisement immediate on his knees; which on thy royal party granted once, his glittering arms he will commend to rust, his barbed steeds to stables, and his heart to faithful service of your majesty.

This swears he, as he is a prince, is just; and as I am a gentleman I credit him.

King Richard II: Northumberland, say thus the king returns, his noble cousin is right welcome hither, and all the number of his fair demands shall be accomplished without contradiction.

With all the gracious utterance thou hast speak to his gentle hearing kind commends.

We do debase ourselves, cousin, do we not.

(To Duke of Aumerle)

To look so poorly and to speak so fair? Shall we call back Northumberland, and send defiance to the traitor, and so die?

Duke of Aumerle: No, good my lord, let's fight with gentle words till time lend friends and friends their helpful swords.

King Richard II: Oh God, Oh God! That ever this tongue of mine that laid the sentence of dread banishment on yon proud man, should take it off again with words of sooth!

Oh that I were as great as is my grief, or lesser than my name!

Or that I could forget what I have been, or not remember what I must be now!

Swell'st thou, proud heart? I'll give thee scope to beat, since foes have scope to beat both thee and me.

Duke of Aumerle: Northumberland comes back from Bolingbroke.

King Richard II: What must the king do now? Must he submit?

The king shall do it: must he be deposed?

The king shall be contented: must he lose the name of king?

Of God's name, let it go, I'll give my jewels for a set of beads; my gorgeous palace for a hermitage, my happy apparel for an almsman's gown, my figured goblets for a dish of wood, my sceptre for a palmer's walking staff, my subjects for a pair of carved saints and my large kingdom for a little grave; a little, little grave, an obscure grave.

Or I'll be buried in the king's highway, some way of common trade, where subjects' feet may hourly trample on their sovereign's head, for on my heart they tread now whilst I live.

And buried once, why not upon my head?

Aumerle, thou weep'st, my tender-hearted cousin!

We'll make foul weather with despised tears;

Our sighs and they shall lodge the summer corn and make a dearth in this revolting land.

Or shall we play the wantons with our woes, and make some pretty match with shedding tears?

As thus, to drop them still upon one place till they have fretted us a pair of graves within the earth and therein lay; there lies two kinsmen digged their graves with weeping eyes.

Would not this ill do well? Well, well, I see I talk but idly, and you laugh at me.

Most mighty prince, my Lord Northumberland, what says King Bolingbroke?

Will his majesty give Richard leave to live till Richard die?

You make a leg, and Bolingbroke says ay.

Earl of Northumberland: My lord, in the base court he doth attend to speak with you; may it please you to come down.

King Richard II: Down, down I come like glistering Phaethon, wanting the manage of unruly jades.

In the base court? Base court, where kings grow base to come at traitors' calls and do them grace.

In the base court? Come down? Down, court! Down, king!

For night-owls shriek where mounting larks should sing.

(Exeunt from above)

Henry IV: What says his majesty?

Earl of Northumberland: Sorrow and grief of heart makes him speak fondly, like a frantic man, yet he is come.

(King Richard and his attendants below enter)

Henry IV: Stand all apart, and show fair duty to his majesty.

(He kneels down)

My gracious lord.

King Richard II: Fair cousin, you debase your princely knee to make the base earth proud with kissing it.

Me rather had my heart might feel your love than my unpleased eye see your courtesy.

Up, cousin, up; your heart is up, I know, thus high at least, although your knee be low.

Henry IV: My gracious lord, I come but for mine own.

King Richard II: Your own is yours, and I am yours, and all.

Henry IV: So far be mine, my most redoubted lord, as my true service shall deserve your love.

King Richard II: Well you deserve: they well deserve to have that know the strong'st and surest way to get.

Uncle, give me your hands: nay, dry your eyes; tears show their love but want their remedies.

Cousin, I am too young to be your father though you are old enough to be my heir.

What you will have, I'll give, and willing too, for do we must what force will have us do.

Set on towards London, cousin, is it so?

Henry IV: Yea, my good Lord:

King Richard II: Then I must not say no.

(Flourishing, Exeunt)

Act III, Scene 4

The Duke of York's garden. Langley.

(The Queen and two Ladies enter)

Queen: What sport shall we devise here in this garden, to drive away the heavy thought of care?

Lady: Madam, we'll play at bowls.

Queen: It will make me think the world is full of rubs, and that my fortune rubs against the bias.

Lady: Madam, we'll dance.

Queen: My legs can keep no measure in delight, when my poor heart no measure keeps in grief; therefore, no dancing girl, some other sport.

Lady: Madam, we'll tell tales.

Queen: Of sorrow or of joy?

Lady: Of either, madam.

Queen: Of neither girl, for of joy, being altogether wanting; it doth remember me the more of sorrow, or if of grief being altogether had; it adds more sorrow to my want of joy.

For what I have I need not to repeat, and what I want it boots not to complain.

Lady: Madam, I'll sing.

Queen: It is well that thou hast cause but thou shouldst please me better, wouldst thou weep.

Lady: I could weep, madam, would it do you good.

Queen: And I could sing, would weeping do me good, nd never borrow any tear of thee.

(A Gardener and two Servants enter)

But stay, here come the gardeners.

Let's step into the shadow of these trees, my wretchedness unto a row of pins, they'll talk of state; for every one doth so against a change; woe is forerun with woe.

(Queen and Ladies retire)

Gardener: Go, bind thou up yon dangling apricocks, which like unruly children make their sire stoop with oppression of their prodigal weight.

Give some supportance to the bending twigs.

Go thou, and like an executioner, cut off the heads of too fast growing sprays that look too lofty in our commonwealth.

All must be even in our government you thus employed, I will go root away the noisome weeds, which without profit suck the soil's fertility from wholesome flowers.

Servant: Why should we in the compass of a pale keep law and form and due proportion, showing, as in a model, our firm estate, when our sea-walled garden, the whole land is full of weeds, her fairest flowers choked up, her fruit-trees all upturned, her hedges ruined, her knots disordered and her wholesome herbs swarming with caterpillars?

Gardener: Hold thy peace, he that hath suffered this disordered spring, hath now himself met with the fall of leaf.

The weeds which his broad-spreading leaves did shelter that seem'd in eating him to hold him up, are plucked up root and all by Bolingbroke, I mean the Earl of Wiltshire, Bushy, Green.

Servant: What, are they dead?

Gardener: They are; and Bolingbroke hath seized the wasteful king.

Oh what pity is it that he had not so trimmed and dressed his land as we this garden!

We at time of year do wound the bark, the skin of our fruit-trees, lest being over-proud in sap and blood with too much riches it confound itself.

Had he done so to great and growing men, they might have lived to bear and he to taste their fruits of duty.

Superfluous branches, we lop away, that bearing boughs may live.

Had he done so, himself had borne the crown, which waste of idle hours hath quite thrown down.

Servant: What, think you then the king shall be deposed?

Gardener: Depressed he is already, and deposed it is doubt he will be: letters came last night to a dear friend of the good Duke of York's that tell black tidings.

Queen: Oh I am pressed to death through want of speaking!

(Coming forward)

Thou, old Adam's likeness, set to dress this garden, how dares thy harsh rude tongue sound this unpleasing news?

What Eve, what serpent, hath suggested thee to make a second fall of cursed man?

Why dost thou say King Richard is deposed?

Darest thou, thou little better thing than earth, divine his downfall? Say, where, when, and how, camest thou by this ill tidings? Speak, thou wretch.

Gardener: Pardon me, madam: little joy have I to breathe this news; yet what I say is true.

King Richard, he is in the mighty hold of Bolingbroke, their fortunes both are weighed.

In your lord's scale is nothing but himself, and some few vanities that make him light, but in the balance of great Bolingbroke.

Besides himself, are all the English peers, and with that odds he weighs King Richard down.

Post you to London, and you will find it so, I speak no more than everyone doth know.

Queen: Nimble mischance, that art so light of foot, doth not thy embassage belong to me, and am I last that knows it?

Oh, thou think'st to serve me last, that I may longest keep thy sorrow in my breast.

Come, ladies, go to meet at London London's king in woe.

What, was I born to this, that my sad look should grace the triumph of great Bolingbroke?

Gardener, for telling me these news of woe, pray God the plants thou graft'st may never grow.

(Exeunt Queen and Ladies)

Gardener: Poor queen! so that thy state might be no worse, I would my skill were subject to thy curse.

Here did she fall a tear, here in this place I'll set a bank of rue, sour herb of grace.

Rue, even for ruth, here shortly shall be seen in the remembrance of a weeping Queen:

(Exeunt)

Act IV, Scene 1

Westminster Hall.

(Henry Bolingbroke, Duke of Aumerle, Northumberland, Henry Percyr, Lord Fitzwater, Duke of Surrey, the Bishop of Carlisle the Abbot of Westminster, and another Lord, Herald, Officers, and Bagot)

Henry IV: Call forth Bagot.

Now, Bagot, freely speak thy mind, what thou dost know of noble Gloucester's death who wrought it with the king, and who performed the bloody office of his timeless end.

Bagot: Then set before my face the Lord Aumerle.

Henry IV: Cousin, stand forth, and look upon that man.

Bagot: My Lord Aumerle, I know your daring tongue scorns to unsay what once it hath delivered.

In that dead time when Gloucester's death was plotted, I heard you say, is not my arm of length that reacheth from the restful English court as far as Calais, to mine uncle's head?'

Amongst much other talk, that very time, I heard you say that you had rather refuse the offer of an hundred thousand crowns than Bolingbroke's return to England; adding withal how blest this land would be in this your cousin's death.

Duke of Aumerle: Princes and noble lords, what answer shall I make to this base man?

Shall I so much dishonour my fair stars, on equal terms to give him chastisement?

Either I must, or have mine honour soiled with the attainder of his slanderous lips.

There is my gage, the manual seal of death, that marks thee out for hell: I say, thou liest, and will maintain what thou hast said is false in thy heart-blood, though being all too base to stain the temper of my knightly sword.

Henry IV: Bagot, forbear, thou shalt not take it up.

Duke of Aumerle: Excepting one, I would he were the best in all this presence that hath moved me so.

Lord Fitzwater: If that thy valour stand on sympathy, there is my gage, Aumerle, in gage to thine.

By that fair sun which shows me where thou stand'st, I heard thee say, and vauntingly thou spakest it that thou wert cause of noble Gloucester's death.

If thou deny'st it twenty times, thou liest; and I will turn thy falsehood to thy heart where it was forged, with my rapier's point.

Duke of Aumerle: Thou darest not, coward, live to see that day.

Lord Fitzwater: Now by my soul, I would it were this hour.

Duke of Aumerle: Fitzwater, thou art damn'd to hell for this.

Hotspur (Henry Percyr): Aumerle, thou liest; his honour is as true in this appeal as thou art all unjust; and that thou art so, there I throw my gage to prove it on thee to the extremest point of mortal breathing, seize it, if thou darest.

Duke of Aumerle: And if I do not, may my hands rot off and never brandish more revengeful steel over the glittering helmet of my foe!

Lord: I task the earth to the like, forsworn Aumerle, and spur thee on with full as many lies as may be hollowed in thy treacherous ear.

From sun to sun: there is my honour's pawn, engage it to the trial if thou darest.

Duke of Aumerle: Who sets me else? By heaven I'll throw at all.

I have a thousand spirits in one breast, to answer twenty thousand such as you.

Duke of Surrey: My Lord Fitzwater, I do remember well the very time Aumerle and you did talk.

Lord Fitzwater: It is very true: you were in presence then, and you can witness with me this is true.

Duke of Surrey: As false, by heaven, as heaven itself is true.

Lord Fitzwater: Surrey, thou liest.

Duke of Surrey: Dishonourable boy!

That lie shall lie so heavy on my sword, that it shall render vengeance and revenge till thou the lie-giver and that lie do lie in earth as quiet as thy father's skull.

In proof whereof, there is my honour's pawn; engage it to the trial if thou darest.

Lord Fitzwater: How fondly dost thou spur a forward horse!

If I dare eat, or drink, or breathe, or live, I dare meet Surrey in a wilderness and spit upon him, whilst I say he lies and lies, and lies.

There is my bond of faith to tie thee to my strong correction, as I intend to thrive in this new world, Aumerle is guilty of my true appeal.

Besides, I heard the banished Norfolk say that thou, Aumerle, didst send two of thy men to execute the noble duke at Calais.

Duke of Aumerle: Some honest Christian trust me with a gage that Norfolk lies, here do I throw down this, if he may be repealed, to try his honour.

Henry IV: These differences shall all rest under gage till Norfolk be repealed, repealed he shall be, and though mine enemy restored again to all his lands and signories.

When he's returned against Aumerle we will enforce his trial.

Bishop of Carlisle: That honourable day shall never be seen.

Many a time hath banished Norfolk fought for Jesus Christ in glorious Christian field, streaming the ensign of the Christian cross against black pagans, Turks, and Saracens.

And toiled with works of war, retired himself to Italy, and there at Venice gave his body to that pleasant country's earth, and his pure soul unto his captain Christ, under whose colours he had fought so long.

Henry IV: Why, bishop, is Norfolk dead?

Bishop of Carlisle: As surely as I live, my Lord.

Henry IV: Sweet peace conduct his sweet soul to the bosom of good old Abraham! Lords appellants,

Your differences shall all rest under gage till we assign you to your days of trial.

(Duke of York enters attended)

Edmund of Langley: Great Duke of Lancaster, I come to thee from plume-plucked Richard; who with willing soul adopts thee heir, and his high sceptre yields to the possession of thy royal hand.

Ascend his throne, descending now from him, and long live Henry, fourth of that name!

Henry IV: In God's name, I'll ascend the regal throne.

Bishop of Carlisle: Marry. God forbid!

Worst in this royal presence may I speak, yet best beseeming me to speak the truth.

Would God that any in this noble presence were enough noble to be upright judge of noble Richard! Then true noblesse would learn him forbearance from so foul a wrong.

What subject can give sentence on his king? And who sits here that is not Richard's subject?

Thieves are not judged but they are by to hear, although apparent guilt be seen in them; and shall the figure of God's majesty, his captain, steward, deputy-elect, anointed, crowned, planted many years, be judged by subject and inferior breath, and he himself not present?

Oh forfend it God, that in a Christian climate souls refined should show so heinous, black, obscene a deed!

I speak to subjects, and a subject speaks, stirred up by God; thus boldly for his king.

My Lord of Hereford here, whom you call king is a foul traitor to proud Hereford's king; and if you crown him, let me prophesy.

The blood of English shall manure the ground, and future ages groan for this foul act; peace shall go sleep with Turks and infidels, and in this seat of peace tumultuous wars shall kin with kin and kind with kind confound; disorder, horror, fear and mutiny shall here inhabit, and this land be called The field of Golgotha and dead men's skulls.

Oh if you raise this house against this house, it will the woefullest division prove that ever fell upon this cursed earth.

Prevent it, resist it, let it not be so, lest child and child's children cry against you woe!

Earl of Northumberland: Well have you argued, sir, and for your pains of capital treason we arrest you here.

My Lord of Westminster, be it your charge to keep him safely till his day of trial.

May it please you, lords, to grant the commons' suit.

Henry IV: Fetch hither Richard, that in common view he may surrender; so we shall proceed without suspicion.

Edmund of Langley: I will be his conduct.

(Exits)

Henry IV: Lords, you that here are under our arrest, procure your sureties for your days of answer.

Little are we beholding to your love, and little looked for at your helping hands.

(Duke of York re-enters with King Richard II, and Officers bearing the regalia)

King Richard II: Alack, why am I sent for to a king, before I have shook off the regal thoughts, wherewith I reigned? I hardly yet have learned to insinuate, flatter, bow, and bend my limbs.

Give sorrow leave awhile to tutor me to this submission.

Yet I well remember the favours of these men: were they not mine?

Did they not sometime cry, all hail! To me?

So Judas did to Christ, but he within twelve, found truth in all but one; I in twelve thousand, none.

God save the king! Will no man say amen?

Am I both priest and clerk? Well then, amen.

God save the king! Although I be not he, and yet amen, if heaven do think him me.

To do what service am I sent for hither?

Edmund of Langley: To do that office of thine own good will which tired majesty did make thee offer the resignation of thy state and crown to Henry Bolingbroke.

King Richard II: Give me the crown.

Here, cousin, seize the crown; here cousin.

On this side my hand, and on that side yours, now is this golden crown like a deep well that owes two buckets, filling one another.

The emptier ever dancing in the air, the other down, unseen and full of water that bucket down and full of tears am I; drinking my griefs, whilst you mount up on high.

Henry IV: I thought you had been willing to resign.

King Richard II: My crown I am; but still my griefs are mine.

You may my glories and my state deposes but not my griefs, still am I king of those.

Henry IV: Part of your cares you give me with your crown.

King Richard II: Your cares set up do not pluck my cares down.

My care is loss of care, by old care done, your care is gain of care by new care won.

The cares I give I have, though given away, they tend the crown yet still with me they stay.

Henry IV: Are you contented to resign the crown?

King Richard II: Ay, no, no, ay, for I must nothing be, therefore no, no, for I resign to thee.

Now mark me, how I will undo myself, I give this heavy weight from off my head and this unwieldy sceptre from my hand, the pride of kingly sway from out my heart; with mine own tears I wash away my balm, with mine own hands I give away my crown, with mine own tongue deny my sacred state, with mine own breath release all duty's rites.

All pomp and majesty I do forswear, my manors, rents, revenues I forego; my acts, decrees, and statutes I deny.

God pardon all oaths that are broke to me!

God keep all vows unbroke that swear to thee!

Make me, that nothing have, with nothing grieved, and thou with all pleased, that hast all achieved!

Long mayst thou live in Richard's seat to sit, and soon lie Richard in an earthly pit!

God save King Harry, unkinged Richard says, and send him many years of sunshine days!

What more remains?

Earl of Northumberland: No more, but that you read these accusations and these grievous crimes committed by your person and your followers against the state and profit of this land; that by confessing them, the souls of men may deem that you are worthily deposed.

King Richard II: Must I do so? And must I ravel out my weaved-up folly?

Gentle Northumberland, if thy offences were upon record would it not shame thee in so fair a troop to read a lecture of them?

If thou wouldst, there shouldst thou find one heinous article containing the deposing of a king and cracking the strong warrant of an oath, marked with a blot, damned in the book of heaven.

Nay, all of you that stand and look upon, whilst that my wretchedness doth bait myself, though some of you with Pilate wash your hands showing an outward pity; yet you Pilates have here delivered me to my sour cross, and water cannot wash away your sin.

Earl of Northumberland: My lord, dispatch, read over these articles.

King Richard II: Mine eyes are full of tears, I cannot see, and yet salt water blinds them not so much but they can see a sort of traitors here.

Nay, if I turn mine eyes upon myself, I find myself a traitor with the rest for I have given here my soul's consent to undeck the pompous body of a king; made glory base and sovereignty a slave proud majesty a subject, state a peasant.

Earl of Northumberland: My lord.

King Richard II: No lord of thine, thou haught insulting man, nor no man's lord; I have no name, no title, no, not that name was given me at the font, but it is usurped.

Alack the heavy day that I have worn so many winters out, and know not now what name to call myself!

Oh that I were a mockery king of snow, standing before the sun of Bolingbroke, to melt myself away in water-drops!

Good king, great king, and yet not greatly good, and if my word be sterling yet in England, let it command a mirror hither straight that it may show me what a face I have; since it is bankrupt of his majesty.

Henry IV: Go some of you and fetch a looking-glass.

(An attesndant exists)

Earl of Northumberland: Read over this paper while the glass doth come.

King Richard II: Fiend, thou torment'st me here, I come to hell!

Henry IV: Urge it no more, my Lord Northumberland.

Earl of Northumberland: The commons will not then be satisfied.

King Richard II: They shall be satisfied, I'll read enough, when I do see the very book indeed where all my sins are written, and that's myself.

(Attendant re-enter with a glass)

Give me the glass, and therein will I read.

No deeper wrinkles yet? Hath sorrow struck so many blows upon this face of mine, and made no deeper wounds?

Oh flattering glass, like to my followers in prosperity, thou dost beguile me!

Was this face the face that every day under his household roof

Did keep ten thousand men? Was this the face that, like the sun, did make beholders wink?

Was this the face that faced so many follies, and was at last out-faced by Bolingbroke?

A brittle glory shineth in this face, As brittle as the glory is the face.

(Dashes the glass against the ground)

For there it is, cracked in a hundred shivers.

Mark, silent king, the moral of this sport, how soon my sorrow hath destroyed my face.

Henry IV: The shadow of your sorrow hath destroyed the shadow or your face.

King Richard II: Say that again.

The shadow of my sorrow! ha! Let's see.

It is very true, my grief lies all within, and these external manners of laments are merely shadows to the unseen grief that swells with silence in the tortured soul; there lies the substance, and I thank thee, king, for thy great bounty, that not only givest me cause to wail but teachest me the way how to lament the cause.

I'll beg one boon, and then be gone and trouble you no more.

Shall I obtain it?

Henry IV: Name it, fair cousin.

King Richard II: Fair cousin? I am greater than a king, for when I was a king, my flatterers were then but subjects, being now a subject I have a king here to my flatterer.

Being so great, I have no need to beg.

Henry IV: Yet ask.

King Richard II: And shall I have?

Henry IV: You shall.

King Richard II: Then give me leave to go.

Henry IV: Whither?

King Richard II: Whither you will, so I were from your sights.

Henry IV: Go, some of you convey him to the Tower.

King Richard II: Oh good! Convey? Conveyers are you all,

That rise thus nimbly by a true king's fall.

(Exeunt King Richard II, some Lords, and a Guard)

Henry IV: On Wednesday next we solemnly set down our coronation, lords, prepare yourselves.

(Exeunt all except the Bishop of Carlisle, the Abbot of Westminster, and Duke of Aumerle)

Abbot: A woeful pageant have we here beheld.

Bishop of Carlisle: The woe's to come; the children yet unborn.

Shall feel this day as sharp to them as thorn.

Duke of Aumerle: You holy clergymen, is there no plot to rid the realm of this pernicious blot?

Abbot: My lord, before I freely speak my mind herein, you shall not only take the sacrament to bury mine intents, but also to effect whatever I shall happen to devise.

I see your brows are full of discontent, your hearts of sorrow and your eyes of tears.

Come home with me to supper, and I'll lay a plot shall show us all a merry day.

(Exeunt)

Act V, Scene 1

A street leading to the Tower. (London)

(Queen and Ladies enter)

Queen: This way the king will come, this is the way **to** Julius Caesar's ill-erected tower, to whose flint bosom my condemned lord is doomed a prisoner by proud Bolingbroke.

Here let us rest, if this rebellious earth, have any resting for her true king's Queen.

(King Richard II and Guard enter)

But soft, but see or rather do not see my fair rose wither, yet look up, behold that you in pity may dissolve to dew; and wash him fresh again with true-love tears.

Ah, thou, the model where old Troy did stand, thou map of honour, thou King Richard's tomb, and not King Richard.

Thou most beauteous inn, why should hard-favoured grief be lodged in thee when triumph is become an alehouse guest?

King Richard II: Join not with grief, fair woman, do not so to make my end too sudden.

Learn, good soul, to think our former state a happy dream; from which awaked, the truth of what we are shows us but this.

I am sworn brother, sweet, to grim Necessity, and he and I will keep a league till death.

Quicken thee to France and cloister thee in some religious house.

Our holy lives must win a new world's crown, which our profane hours here have stricken down.

Queen: What, is my Richard both in shape and mind transformed and weakened?

Hath Bolingbroke deposed thine intellect? Hath he been in thy heart?

The lion dying thrusteth forth his paw, and wounds the earth, if nothing else with rage to be overpowered; and wilt thou, pupil-like, take thy correction mildly, kiss the rod and fawn on rage with base humility; which art a lion and a king of beasts?

King Richard II: A king of beasts, indeed, if aught but beasts, I had been still a happy king of men.

Good sometime queen, prepare thee hence for France.

Think I am dead and that even here thou takest, as from my death-bed, thy last living leave.

In winter's tedious nights sit by the fire with good old folks and let them tell thee tales of woeful ages long ago betid; and here thou bid good night to quit their griefs,

Tell thou the lamentable tale of me and send the hearers weeping to their beds.

For why, the senseless brands will sympathize the heavy accent of thy moving tongue and in compassion weep the fire out; and some will mourn in ashes, some coal-black, for the deposing of a rightful king.

(Northumberland and others enter)

Earl of Northumberland: My lord, the mind of Bolingbroke is changed.

You must to Pomfret, not unto the Tower and, madam, there is order taken for you with all swift speed you must away to France.

King Richard II: Northumberland, thou ladder wherewithal the mounting Bolingbroke ascends my throne; the time shall not be many hours of age more than it is here foul sin gathering head shalt break into corruption.

Thou shalt think, though he divide the realm and give thee half; it is too little, helping him to all, and he shall think that thou which know'st the way to plant unrightful kings, wilt know again, being ne'er so little urged, another way to pluck him headlong from the usurped throne.

The love of wicked men converts to fear, that fear to hate, and hate turns one or both you worthy danger and deserved death.

Earl of Northumberland: My guilt be on my head, and there an end.

Take leave and part; for you must part forthwith.

King Richard II: Doubly divorced! Bad men, you violate a twofold marriage, it were my crown and me, and then between me and my married wife.

Let me unkiss the oath it was thee and me; and yet not so, for with a kiss it was made. part us, Northumberland, I toward the north, where shivering cold and sickness pines the clime; my wife to France: from whence, set forth in pomp, she came adorned hither like sweet May, sent back like Hallowmas or short'st of day.

Queen: And must we be divided? Must we part?

King Richard II: Ay, hand from hand, my love, and heart from heart.

Queen: Banish us both and send the king with me.

Earl of Northumberland: That were some love but little policy.

Queen: Then whither he goes, thither let me go.

King Richard II: So two, together weeping, make one woe.

Weep thou for me in France, I for thee here; better far off than near, be never the near.

Go, count thy way with sighs, I mine with groans.

Queen: So longest way shall have the longest moans.

King Richard II: Twice for one step I'll groan, the way being short, and piece the way out with a heavy heart.

Come, come, in wooing sorrow let's be brief, since wedding it there is such length in grief; one kiss shall stop our mouths, and dumbly part; thus give I mine, and thus take I thy heart.

Queen: Give me mine own again; it were no good part to take on me to keep and kill thy heart.

So, now I have mine own again, be gone, that I might strive to kill it with a groan.

King Richard II: We make woe wanton with this fond delay once more, adieu.

The rest let sorrow say.

(Exeunt)

Act V, Scene 2

The Duke of York's palace.

(Duke of York and Duchess of York enter)

Duchess of York: My lord, you told me you would tell the rest, when weeping made you break the story off of our two cousins coming into London.

Edmund of Langley: Where did I leave?

Duchess of York: At that sad stop, my lord, where rude misgoverned hands from windows' tops threw dust and rubbish on King Richard's head.

Edmund of Langley: Then, as I said, the duke, great Bolingbroke, mounted upon a hot and fiery steed, which his aspiring rider seemed to know; with slow but stately pace kept on his course.

Whilst all tongues cried God save thee, Bolingbroke!'

You would have thought the very windows spake so many greedy looks of young and old through casements darted their desiring eyes upon his visage, and that all the walls with painted imagery had said at once, Jesus preserve thee!

Welcome, Bolingbroke!' Whilst he, from the one side to the other turning bareheaded, lower than his proud steed's neck, bespake them thus: I thank you, countrymen.

And thus still doing, thus he passed along Duchess of York; alas, poor Richard!

Where rode he the whilst?

Edmund of Langley: As in a theatre, the eyes of men, after a well-graced actor leaves the stage, are idly bent on him that enters next,

Thinking his prattle to be tedious, even so, or with much more contempt in men's eye did scowl on gentle Richard; no man cried God save him!

No joyful tongue gave him his welcome home, but dust was thrown upon his sacred head, which with such gentle sorrow he shook off, his face still combating with tears and smiles the badges of his grief and patience that had not God, for some strong purpose, steeled the hearts of men, they must perforce have melted and barbarism itself have pitied him.

But heaven hath a hand in these events, to whose high will we bound our calm contents.

To Bolingbroke are we sworn subjects now, whose state and honour I for aye allow.

Duchess of York: Here comes my son Aumerle.

Edmund of Langley: Aumerle that was, but that is lost for being Richard's friend, and, madam, you must call him Rutland now.

I am in parliament pledge for his truth and lasting fealty to the new-made king.

(Duke of Aumerle enters)

Duchess of York: Welcome, my son: who are the violets now that strew the green lap of the new come spring?

Duke of Aumerle: Madam, I know not nor I greatly care not, God knows I had as life be none as one.

Edmund of Langley: Well, bear you well in this new spring of time, lest you be cropped before you come to prime.

What news from Oxford? Hold those justs and triumphs?

Duke of Aumerle: For aught I know, my lord, they do.

Edmund of Langley: You will be there, I know.

Duke of Aumerle: If God prevent not, I purpose so.

Edmund of Langley: What seal is that, that hangs without thy bosom?

Yea, look'st thou pale? Let me see the writing.

Duke of Aumerle: My lord, 'tis nothing.

Edmund of Langley: No matter then who see it, I will be satisfied; let me see the writing.

Duke of Aumerle: I do beseech your grace to pardon me, it is a matter of small consequence, which for some reasons I would not have seen.

Edmund of Langley: Which for some reasons, sir, I mean to see.

I fear, I fear, Duchess of York, what should you fear?

It is nothing but some bond that he is entered into for happy apparel against the triumph day.

Edmund of Langley: Bound to himself! What doth he with a bond that he is bound to? Wife, thou art a fool.

Boy, let me see the writing.

Duke of Aumerle: I do beseech you, pardon me; I may not show it.

Edmund of Langley: I will be satisfied, let me see it, I say.

(He plucks it out of his bosom and reads it)

Treason! Foul treason! Villain! Traitor! Slave!

Duchess of York: What is the matter, my lord?

Edmund of Langley: Oh! Who is within there?

(Enter a Servant)

Saddle my horse.

God for his mercy, what treachery is here!

Duchess of York: Why, what is it, my lord?

Edmund of Langley: Give me my boots, I say, saddle my horse.

Now, by mine honour, by my life, by my troth, I will appeach the villain.

Duchess of York: What is the matter?

Edmund of Langley: Peace, foolish woman.

Duchess of York: I will not peace.

What is the matter, Aumerle.

Duke of Aumerle: Good mother, be content; it is no more than my poor life must answer.

Duchess of York: Thy life answer!

Edmund of Langley: Bring me my boots: I will unto the king.

(Servant re-enters with boots)

Duchess of York: Strike him, Aumerle.

Poor boy, thou art amazed.

Hence, villain! Never more come in my sight.

Edmund of Langley: Give me my boots, I say.

Duchess of York: Why, York, what wilt thou do?

Wilt thou not hide the trespass of thine own?

Have we more sons? Or are we like to have?

Is not my teeming date drunk up with time?

And wilt thou pluck my fair son from mine age, and rob me of a happy mother's name?

Is he not like thee? Is he not thine own?

Edmund of Langley: Thou fond mad woman, wilt thou conceal this dark conspiracy?

A dozen of them here have taken the sacrament, and interchangeably set down their hands to kill the king at Oxford.

Duchess of York: He shall be none, we'll keep him here; then what is that to him?

Edmund of Langley: Away, fond woman! Were he twenty times my son, I would appeach him.

Duchess of York: Hadst thou groaned for him as I have done, thou wouldst be more pitiful.

But now I know thy mind; thou dost suspect that I have been disloyal to thy bed, and that he is a bastard, not thy son.

Sweet York, sweet husband, be not of that mind.

He is as like thee as a man may be, not like to me, or any of my kin, and yet I love him.

Edmund of Langley: Make way, unruly woman!

(Exits)

Duchess of York: After, Aumerle! Mount thee upon his horse; spur post and get before him to the king, and beg thy pardon ere he do accuse thee.

I'll not be long behind; though I be old, I doubt not but to ride as fast as York.

And never will I rise up from the ground till Bolingbroke have pardoned thee.

Away, be gone!

(Exeunt)

Act V, Scene 3

A royal palace.

(Henry Bolingbroke, Henry Percyr, and other Lords enter)

Henry IV: Can no man tell me of my unthrifty son?

I is full three months since I did see him last, if any plague hang over us, it is he.

I would to God, my lords, he might be found.

Inquire at London, amongst the taverns there, for there, they say he daily doth frequent with unrestrained loose companions, even such they say as stands in narrow lanes, and beat our watch, and rob our passengers; which he, young wanton and effeminate boy, takes on the point of honour to support, so dissolute a crew.

Hotspur (Henry Percyr): My lord, some two days since I saw the prince, and told him of those triumphs held at Oxford.

Henry IV: And what said the gallant?

Hotspur (Henry Percyr): His answer was, he would unto the stews, and from the common'st creature pluck a glove, and wear it as a favour; and with that he would unhorse the lustiest challenger.

Henry IV: As dissolute as desperate; yet through both I see some sparks of better hope, which elder years may happily bring forth. But who comes here?

(Duke of Aumerle enters)

Duke of Aumerle: Where is the king?

Henry IV: What means our cousin, that he stares and looks so wildly?

Duke of Aumerle: God save your grace! I do beseech your majesty, to have some conference with your grace alone.

Henry IV: Withdraw yourselves, and leave us here alone.

(Exeunt Henry Percyr and Lords)

What is the matter with our cousin now?

Duke of Aumerle: For ever may my knees grow to the earth, my tongue cleaves to my roof within my mouth unless a pardon here I rise or speak.

Henry IV: Intended or committed was this fault?

If on the first, how heinous ever it be, to win thy after-love I pardon thee.

Duke of Aumerle: Then give me leave that I may turn the key, that no man enters till my tale be done.

Henry IV: Have thy desire.

Edmund of Langley: **(Within)** My liege beware, look to thyself, thou hast a traitor in thy presence there.

Henry IV: Villain, I'll make thee safe.

(Drawing)

Duke of Aumerle: Stay thy revengeful hand; thou hast no cause to fear.

Edmund of Langley: **(Within)** Open the door, secure, foolhardy king.

Shall I for love speak treason to thy face? Open the door, or I will break it open.

(Duke of York enters)

Henry IV: What is the matter, uncle? Speak, recover breath, tell us how near is danger, that we may arm us to encounter it.

Edmund of Langley: Peruse this writing here, and thou shalt know the treason that my haste forbids me show.

Duke of Aumerle: Remember, as thou read'st, thy promise passed.

I do repent me; read not my name there my heart is not confederate with my hand.

Edmund of Langley: It was, villain, were thy hand did set it down.

I tore it from the traitor's bosom king, fear and not love begets his penitence.

Forget to pity him, lest thy pity prove a serpent that will sting thee to the heart.

Henry IV: Oh heinous, strong, and bold conspiracy!

Oh loyal father of a treacherous son!

Thou sheer, immaculate and silver fountain, from when this stream through muddy passages hath held his current and defiled himself!

Thy overflow of good converts to bad, and thy abundant goodness shall excuse this deadly blot in thy digressing son.

Edmund of Langley: So shall my virtue be his vice's bawd, and he shall spend mine honour with his shame as thriftless sons their scraping fathers' gold.

Mine honour lives when his dishonour dies, or my shamed life in his dishonour lies.

Thou kill'st me in his life; giving him breath, the traitor lives, the true man's put to death.

Duchess of York: (Within) What ho, my liege! For God's sake, let me in.

Henry IV: What shrill-voiced suppliant makes this eager cry?

Duchess of York: A woman and thy aunt, great king, it is I; speak with me, pity me, open the door.

A beggar begs that never begged before.

Henry IV: Our scene is altered from a serious thing, and now changed to the Beggar and the King.

My dangerous cousin, let your mother in; I know she is come to pray for your foul sin.

Edmund of Langley: If thou do pardon, whosoever pray, more sins for this forgiveness prosper may.

This festered joint cut off, the rest rest sound; this let alone will all the rest confound.

(Duchess of York enter)

Duchess of York: Oh king, believe not this hard-hearted man!

Love loving not itself none other can.

Edmund of Langley: Thou frantic woman, what dost thou make here?

Shall thy old dugs once more a traitor rear?

Duchess of York: Sweet York, be patient.

Hear me, gentle liege.

(Kneels)

Henry IV: Rise up, good aunt.

Duchess of York: Not yet, I thee beseech.

For ever will I walk upon my knees, and never see day that the happy sees, till thou give joy; until thou bid me joy by pardoning Rutland, my transgressing boy.

Duke of Aumerle: Unto my mother's prayers I bend my knee.

Edmund of Langley: Against them both my true joints bended be.

Ill mayst thou thrive, if thou grant any grace!

Duchess of York: Pleads he in earnest?

Look upon his face, his eyes do drop no tears, his prayers are in jest; his words come from his mouth, ours from our breast.

He prays but faintly and would be denied, we pray with heart and soul and all beside.

His weary joints would gladly rise, I know, our knees shall kneel till to the ground they grow.

His prayers are full of false hypocrisy, ours if of true zeal and deep integrity.

Our prayers do out-pray his, then let them have that mercy which true prayer ought to have.

Henry IV: Good aunt, stand up.

Duchess of York: Nay, do not say, stand up; say pardon first, and afterwards stand up.

And if I were thy nurse, thy tongue to teach, Pardon should be the first word of thy speech.

I never longed to hear a word till now, say pardon king, let pity teach thee how the word is short, but not so short as sweet; no word like pardon' for kings mouths so meet.

Edmund of Langley: Speak it in French, king, say pardon me.

Duchess of York: Dost thou teach pardon pardon to destroy?

Ah, my sour husband, my hard-hearted lord, that set'st the word itself against the word!

Speak pardon as it is current in our land, the chopping French we do not understand.

Thine eye begins to speak; set thy tongue there, or in thy piteous heart plant thou thine ear; that hearing how our plaints and prayers do pierce, pity may move thee pardon to rehearse.

Henry IV: Good aunt, stand up.

Duchess of York: I do not sue to stand, pardon is all the suit I have in hand.

Henry IV: I pardon him, as God shall pardon me.

Duchess of York: Oh happy vantage of a kneeling knee!

Yet am I sick for fear: speak it again, twice saying pardon doth not pardon twain; but makes one pardon strong.

Henry IV: With all my heart I pardon him.

Duchess of York: A god on earth thou art.

Henry IV: But for our trusty brother-in-law and the abbot, with all the rest of that consorted crew, destruction straight shall dog them at the heels.

Good uncle, help to order several powers to Oxford, or wherever these traitors are, they shall not live within this world, I swear, but I will have them if I once know where.

Uncle, farewell.

And, cousin too, adieu.

Your mother well hath prayed, and prove you true.

Duchess of York: Come, my old son: I pray God make thee new.

(Exeunt)

Act V, Scene 4

(Exton and Servant enter)

Sir Pierce of Exton: Didst thou not mark the king, what words he spake, have I no friend will rid me of this living fear?'

Was it not so?

Servant: These were his very words.

Sir Pierce of Exton: Have I no friend? Quoth he, he spake it twice, and urged it twice together, did he not?

Servant: He did.

Sir Pierce of Exton: And speaking it, he wistly looked on me, and who should say; I would thou wert the man that would divorce this terror from my heart, meaning the king at Pomfret. Come, let's go.

I am the king's friend, and will rid his foe.

(Exeunt)

Act V, Scene 5

Pomfret castle.

(King Richard enters)

King Richard II: I have been studying how I may compare this prison where I live unto the world.

And for because the world is populous, and here is not a creature but myself, I cannot do it; yet I'll hammer it out.

My brain I'll prove the female to my soul, my soul the father; and these two beget a generation of still-breeding thoughts, and these same thoughts people this little world; in humours like the people of this world for no thought is contented.

The better sort, as thoughts of things divine are intermixed with scruples and do set the word itself against the word.

As thus, come little ones, and then again, it is as hard to come as for a camel to thread the postern of a small needle's eye.

Thoughts tending to ambition, they do plot unlikely wonders how these vain weak nails may tear a passage through the flinty ribs of this hard world, my ragged prison walls, and, for they cannot die in their own pride.

Thoughts tending to content flatter themselves that they are not the first of fortune's slaves, nor shall not be the last; like silly beggars who sitting in the stocks refuge their shame, that many have and others must sit there.

In this thought they find a kind of ease, bearing their own misfortunes on the back of such as have before endured the like.

Thus play I in one person many people, and none contented, sometimes am I king; then treasons make me wish myself a beggar, and so I am.

Then crushing penury persuades me I was better when a king, then am I kinged again, and by and by think that I am unkinged by Bolingbroke, and straight am nothing.

But whatever I be, nor I nor any man that but man is with nothing shall be pleased, till he be eased with being nothing.

Music do I hear?

(Music)

Ha, ha! Keep time, how sour sweet music is when time is broke and no proportion kept!

So is it in the music of men's lives.

And here have I the daintiness of ear to cheque time broke in a disorder'd string, but for the concord of my state and time had not an ear to hear my true time broke.

I wasted time, and now doth time waste me;

For now hath time made me his numbering clock, my thoughts are minutes, and with sighs they jar their watches on unto mine eyes, the outward watch whereto my finger like a dial's point.

Is pointing still, in cleansing them from tears, now sir the sound that tells what hour it is are clamorous groans, which strike upon my heart, which is the bell; so sighs and tears and groans, show minutes, times, and hours.

But my time runs posting on in Bolingbroke's proud joy, while I stand fooling here, his Jack o' the clock.

This music maddens me, let it sound no more, for though it have help madmen to their wits; in me it seems it will make wise men mad.

Yet blessing on his heart that gives it me!

For it is a sign of love; and love to Richard is a strange brooch in this all-hating world.

(A Groom of the Stable enters)

Groom: Hail, royal prince!

King Richard II: Thanks, noble peer, the cheapest of us is ten groats too dear.

What art thou? And how comest thou hither, where no man never comes but that sad dog that brings me food to make misfortune live?

Groom: I was a poor groom of thy stable, king, when thou wert king; who, travelling towards York, with much ado at length have gotten leave to look upon my sometimes royal master's face.

Oh how it yearned my heart when I beheld in London streets, that coronation-day, when Bolingbroke rode on roan Barbary, that horse that thou so often hast bestrid, that horse that I so carefully have dressed!

King Richard II: Rode he on Barbary? Tell me, gentle friend, how went he under him?

Groom: So proudly as if he disdained the ground.

King Richard II: So proud that Bolingbroke was on his back!

That jade hath eat bread from my royal hand, this hand hath made him proud with clapping him.

Would he not stumble? Would he not fall down since pride must have a fall, and break the neck of that proud man that did usurp his back?

Forgiveness, horse! Why do I rail on thee, since thou created to be awed by man wast born to bear? I was not made a horse.

And yet I bear a burthen like an ass, spurred, galled and tired by jouncing Bolingbroke.

(Keeper enters with a dish)

Keeper: Fellow, give place; here is no longer stay.

King Richard II: If thou love me, 'tis time thou wert away.

Groom: What my tongue dares not, that my heart shall say.

(Exits)

Keeper: My lord, will it please you to fall to?

King Richard II: Taste of it first, as thou art wont to do.

Keeper: My lord, I dare not: Sir Pierce of Exton, who lately came from the king, commands the contrary.

King Richard II: The devil take Henry of Lancaster and thee! Patience is stale, and I am weary of it.

(Beats the keeper)

Keeper: Help, help, help!

(Exton and Servants enter armed)

King Richard II: How now! What means death in this rude assault?

Villain, thy own hand yields thy death's instrument.

(Snatching an axe from a Servant and killing him)

Go thou, and fill another room in hell.

(He kills another. Then Exton strikes him down)

That hand shall burn in never-quenching fire that staggers thus my person.

Exton, thy fierce hand hath with the king's blood stained the king's own land.

Mount, mount, my soul! Thy seat is up on high, whilst my gross flesh sinks downward, here to die.

(Dies)

Sir Pierce of Exton: As full of valour as of royal blood.

Both have I spilled, Oh would the deed were good!

For now the devil, that told me I did well says that this deed is chronicled in hell.

This dead king to the living king I'll bear; take hence the rest, and give them burial here.

(Exeunt)

Act V, Scene 6

Windsor castle.

(Flourishing)

(Henry Bolingbroke, Duke of York, with other Lords, and Attendants enter)

Henry IV: Kind uncle York, the latest news we hear is that the rebels have consumed with fire.

Our town of Cicester in Gloucestershire, but whether they be taken or slain we hear not.

(Northunberland enters)

Welcome my Lord, what is the news?

Earl of Northumberland: First, to thy sacred state wish I all happiness.

The next news is, I have to London sent the heads of Oxford, Salisbury, Blunt, and Kent; the manner of their taking may appear at large discoursed in this paper here.

Henry IV: We thank thee, gentle Percy, for thy pains, and to thy worth will add right worthy gains.

(Lord Fitzwater enters)

Lord Fitzwater: My lord, I have from Oxford sent to London

The heads of Brocas and Sir Bennet Seely, two of the dangerous consorted traitors that sought at Oxford thy dire overthrow.

Henry IV: Thy pains, Fitzwater, shall not be forgotten, right noble is thy merit, well I know.

(Henry Percyr, and the Bishop of Carlisle)

Hotspur (Henry Percyr): The grand conspirator, Abbot of Westminster, with clog of conscience and sour melancholy hath yielded up his body to the grave; but here is Carlisle living, to abide thy kingly doom and sentence of his pride.

Henry IV: Carlisle, this is your doom, choose out some secret place, some reverend room, more than thou hast, and with it joy thy life; so as thou livest in peace die free from strife.

For though mine enemy thou hast ever been, high sparks of honour in thee have I seen.

(Exton enters with persons bearing a coffin)

Sir Pierce of Exton: Great king, within this coffin I present thy buried fear: herein all breathless lies the mightiest of thy greatest enemies, Richard of Bordeaux, by me hither brought.

Henry IV: Exton, I thank thee not; for thou hast wrought a deed of slander with thy fatal hand upon my head and all this famous land.

Sir Pierce of Exton: From your own mouth, my lord, did I this deed.

Henry IV: They love not poison that do poison need, nor do I thee.

Though I did wish him dead, I hate the murderer, love him murdered.

The guilt of conscience take thou for thy labour, but neither my good word nor princely favour.

With Cain go wander through shades of night, and never show thy head by day nor light.

Lords, I protest, my soul is full of woe, that blood should sprinkle me to make me grow; come, mourn with me for that I do lament, and put on sullen black incontinent.

I'll make a voyage to the Holy Land, to wash this blood off from my guilty hand.

March sadly after; grace my mournings here in weeping after this untimely bier.

(Exeunt)

The End

Description of Titles

The Comedy of Errors
Caught in a land of embittered woman and war, caught in months of strife, where a merchant's visit offers little natural relief. The fleeting moment of approving gold, inspire further bitterness, upon an approach to the marketplace, and then the women that occupy within them.

19 Characters

The Taming of the Shrew
Arrangements are made to spencer would be suiters to melt the splendors of a strong willed women. The winning is found pledged, influencing maids to seek their turns, and meanwhile terms required, an authentic spirit that they will/would wed soon.

34 Characters

Love's Labor's Lost
The house of a scholarly pursuit, returns into an expressive, either poetic or drunken as highlighting the gold-slur filled house of charms and dance like rhymes

19 Characters

A Midsummer Night's Dream
Journey into a land of fairies, where creatures are found to have the same issues as nobilities. Exemplifying, perhaps, there's no place like home. Meet fairies as they frolic and play the noble hearts and sway, posed in the recesses of night, and mystic lands of a faraway kingdom.

22 Characters

The Merchant of Venice

An angry Shylock brings to trial a merchant, over a lover's quarrel disrupted, demanding pounds of flesh. With no desires for even three times the amount, the Shylock demands his vengeance at heart.

22 Characters

The Merry Wives of Windsor
Mistresses and lords try and relate towards one another, as various important community figures come to have their word/seek the hostesses. Pleasantries are exchanged as a range of charms are expressed, until conversation resembled so to folly.

23 Characters

Much Ado About Nothing
Soldiery level consideration occupy the gossip, as several hostilities are summoned up, onto heart related matter. Also in conflict. The latter portion of the story lightens up to a women's home and pleasantries. Thereafter, a general search and care in actions, creating response phrasing poetic to the responses of leadership parading, until an end full of sensitivity asking gently questions, onto kisses

23 Characters

As You Like It
Troubled lower nobles venture about daily business, with some mild graces towards the ladies found. In need of relief or play, the Duke and family members take to the woods, where jests of drinking turn into troubled amusements, or warmth of a women's heart.

26 Characters

Troilus and Cressida
The infamous Greek battle for Troy. A large army arrives to take back the lost love of a humiliated foe. Both sides mobilize heroes onto the field, as soldiers and generals move to the side, and let strategies and fate take their course.

21+ Characters

All's Well That Ends Well
A tale of delightful, womanly gossip of a prestigious sort, until the French King has his word on the excellence of others. The story initially revolves around a strong willed countess, whose courteous pose and insight, reflect a nobility reflective of the house and court (council). Dialogue therein revolving around the councils rather, to exemplify (court counselling women).

25 Characters

Measure for Measure
Statesmen discourse leading with time to a personal reflection. Strolling Dukes and strong willed women occupy the background, where high-function status and family discourse intertwine within formalities (of administrative foresight, expression) observed.

24 Characters

Richard III
An in palace drama with King Richard the 3rd, Queen Elizabeth, and Queen Margret. Onto a haunting reunion, as the state processes royal executions.

61+ Characters

The Life and Death of King John
King John and Queen Elinor entertain the royal court, where a bastard has come to make his day. Strategic deployments of influence are exemplified, as the bastard plots about until alerts, alarm corruption has delivered trouble makers known.

24 Characters

Romeo and Juliet
Lovers emerge within a city gripped with two feuding houses apposed. As turmoil are caught in bitter heat, the lover's. Bliss and undying pledge becomes them, onto the eternal soul (of love and romance).

33 Characters

Othello
A hopeful Othello calls upon the favor of allies based on proposed merits, which called upon allies and foes to him. In a mixed response, allies and foes campaign both against Othello, becoming a bitter, personal tangle over a mislead love adventure representing the future of either fates

25 Characters

Macbeth
A desperate Macbeth ventures towards witches to tell fortune, returning to a castle haunted by ghost/old-spirits. Macbeth's worries become frightful nightmares, along the despair of the household around him.

39 Characters

Mark Antony and Cleopatra
The relations or affections of Mark Anthony and Cleopatra, onto the strategic interactions between Mark Anthony and Octavius. The discourse moves to the Octavius house, revealing Octavia, and later then, Pompey in the background. Overall the focus retains upon Mark Anthony, Cleopatra, and Octavius.

56+ Characters

Coriolanus
Citizens riot during a famine, while the state administrative intervenes and otherwise discourses the seriousness of the matter and war. Lady's calm the general ambience, until the sword is mobilized to defend the gates, , while the plight of people is nevertheless heard convincing Roman elites the problem is being found/fought within.

60 Characters

Pericles Prince of Tyre
A thoughtful/reflective Pericles interposes his good will and well-meaning nature, which leads him to visit fishermen friends, and onto state function. Pericles is then confronted, required to (take a plunge) to marry, embedding him deeper into ocean stock of sea life among sailors experience and merchant owners, investing his interest as babe, securing his destiny as then, future king

44 Characters

Cymbeline
Cymbeline, friend or loyalist to the first Caesars, is summoned into battle. Meanwhile there are personal matters to attend to within the noble house.

41 Characters

The Winter's Tale
A gossipy tale of high office, administrative daily insight onto the tender meaning of things and people an how they unite unwittingly at the discourse of their respected hierarchies of partnership. Profoundness therein inspiring the recounts of clown and child, as examples perhaps of what state administration and or nobility's company keeps.

34+ Characters

The Tempest
After an earth shattering storm, a fairy dwelling world is found. There magic and graces are there in song, glory and praises.

21 Characters

The Two Gentlemen of Verona
Loving beginnings, yet far too. General virtues going upwards in hierarchies, with overall chivalrous wits.

Twelfth Night
An evening in the company of sound gatherings, seemingly a docile manner recount version of noble delights. In similarities of the pose, composing an environment of insight and oversight.

Henry the 8th
Across chamber and palace, Dukes and lords, until Queen Katharine's and King Henry VIII's present their graces, conversing the Cardinal then. The signs then, an Elizabeth is born.

Richard II
King Richard the 2nd readies the armed forces at the sound of alarm, while later Henry IV is near for discussion. King Richard the 2nd and his groom.

Henry V
King Henry the 5th, as found across his palace, until a readiness for war. King Henry the 5th and the French King, with armies both have at it.

Henry VI, Part 1
Funeral of King Henry the 5th, Henry VI makes his approach to France. Henry VI fashions as thy lord protector.

Henry VI, Part 2
King Henry the 6th, where the Cardinal is seen mocking protectors with praise, as all the rage. Queen Margaret at King Henry VI, until the end.

Henry VI, Part 3
King Henry VI is busy fighting a succession of battles, France and England as having at it, yet again.

King Henry the 5th
King Henry 5 fight his way toward France, they reach the peaceful and loving responses of a French King.

Henry IV, Part 1
King Henry the 4th, from Palace to Pub, onto the battle fields again. Until there is no rebellion.

Henry IV, Part 2
Henry IV, from Palace, Priest and then tavern, he nevertheless finds some peace, after reflection. King Henry IV, and then King Henry V as fashionable by the end.

Titus Andronicus
A story of Romans and Goths, where roman sways give way. And then to see about Goths and proving worthiness.

28 Characters

Julius Caesar
Near the Final days of the 1st Caesar, and the continuation everlasting as through Octavius.

Hamlet
Hamlet, and his father the King, the father yet a Ghost. Hamlet, not so eager to join.

King Lear
King Lear, from palace to castle, to fighting the French in the field. After battle King Lear is in bed, the Doctor discourses, what lays then now, will have an impact upon the end.

Timon of Athens
A story set in Greece, a place of poets and cultured, good graces. From Arts and daily expressive, to political and charmed.

www.ingramcontent.com/pod-product-compliance
Lightning Source LLC
Chambersburg PA
CBHW071453080526
44587CB00014B/2093